An Educator's Guide to Working with African American Students (4th Edition)

by:

Chance W. Lewis, Ph.D.
Carol Grotnes Belk Distinguished Professor of Urban Education

Director, The Urban Education Collaborative
College of Education

The University of North Carolina at Charlotte

E-mail: chance.lewis@gmail.com
Web: http://www.chancewlewis.com

ISBN: 9781082572999

Published by:

Lewis Educational Consultants, Inc.
Phone: (704) 659-6842
Fax: (866) 370.2642
Web: http://www.chancewlewis.com
E-mail: chance.lewis@gmail.com

*Cover Art photo credit: U.S. Department of Education
Photo used under the Creative Commons License Agreement

TABLE OF CONTENTS

Dedication

This book is dedicated to my grandparents, Mr. Lloyd O. Lewis, Sr.; Mrs. Peggy Lewis; Mrs. K. Frances Thomas and Dr. W. W. Clem. All of whom planted a seed of greatness down in me that, over time, flourished while they were here on earth. Thank you for nurturing the seed of greatness!

This book is also dedicated to my two daughters, Myra Nicole Lewis and Sydney Camille Lewis. It is my hope that Daddy has shown you an example of how hard work can pay off for your benefit if you continue to work hard and stay focused on your goals. It has been such a joy to see both of you grow up so fast. Always remember that Daddy loves you very much and prays for you to reach your full potential. Please know that Daddy will always be there for you. I ask that you carry on all the positive things that you have learned in life. I am so proud of each of you.

Acknowledgements

I want to thank my Lord and Savior Jesus Christ. I want to thank You for the opportunity to write the 4th edition of this important book and allowing me to untangle and crystallize some of the many thoughts I have in my head. It is only because of You that I can now write books after being told that writing was not my gift. It is absolutely amazing how you allow my weakness to become my strength. I continue to learn in this life that it doesn't matter what others say as long as you are pleased with my life. Thank you for guiding me in the way you wanted me to go when so many others had their own opinions of what I should be doing. This is the inspiration that keeps me moving forward every day with a constant focus on reaching my full potential.

I want to thank my wife, Mechael B. Lewis and my daughters Myra Nicole Lewis and Sydney Camille Lewis for allocating the room and space for me to complete this monumental project. You are my inspiration as I continue to write and push forward in trying to make a difference in the world. Each time I look at each of you I continue to get a new motivation to be the best that I can be. Thank you for the sacrifice of time that allows me to reach my full potential. It is my hope that my work ethic will push my daughters to life up to their full potential as well. I love you very much!

I also want to acknowledge my mother, Mrs. Brenda C. Davis, a master educator, who gave me the essential tools to become a great educator. Can you believe it? We have moved from teaching in a high school classroom next door to each other to informing the world about education. You had this vision of my potential a long time ago. I thank you for all the sacrifices over the years. Only a mother's love and prayers got me through. I love you very much!

Additionally, I want to acknowledge my Uncle Miland who always was there for me. You are a big part of my success and have been a great role model to me. I want to thank my best friends Demond Turner, Thomas 'Tommy J' Hutcherson and Timothy Wallace. You all have been 'real' friends over the years and I value all of our life experiences together.

I want to thank all of my Pastors that have poured into me over the years: Pastor George W.C. Calvin; Pastor Roger Lathan; Pastor Darlene Moore; Pastor David Williams, Pastor Kris Erskine, Pastor Marie Nutall and Pastor Ralph McCormick. Your spiritual guidance has been monumental in my spiritual development to navigate this journey called life.

Finally, I want to thank all of my students that I taught in high school, community college and the university level over the years. I have learned so much for each of you. It is my hope that I have done something to plant a 'seed of greatness' inside of you. It is my hope that all of you take something that you have learned and use it to become a positive influence in the lives of others. Pay it forward!

The Writing Style

For the 4th Edition of this book, I continue to deliberately write in the 'first person' voice although the majority of my work in the "ivory tower" of higher education, because of the writing parameters, are in an academic 'third person' voice. However, because I am gearing this book to educational practitioners (i.e., teachers, counselors, and administrators, etc.) in K-12 educational settings, I chose to make my writing style more personal to the reader to have maximum effect for African American students in K-12 schools.

Other Books/Resources by Chance W. Lewis, Ph.D.

White Teachers/Diverse Classrooms: A Guide for Building Inclusive Schools, Promoting High Expectations and Eliminating Racism
(Stylus Publishing, 2006)

White Teachers/Diverse Classrooms: Teachers and Students of Color Talk Candidly about Connecting with Black Students and Transforming Educational Outcomes (DVD)
(Stylus Publishers, 2007)

The Dilemmas of Being an African American Male in the New Millennium: Solutions for Life Transformation
(Infinity Publishing, 2008)

An Educator's Guide to Working with African American Students: Strategies for Promoting Academic Success (First Edition),
(Infinity Publishing, 2009)

Transforming Teacher Education: What Went Wrong and How Can We Fix It
(Stylus Publishing, 2010)

White Teachers/Diverse Classrooms: Creating Inclusive Schools, Building on Students' Diversity and Providing True Educational Equity
(Stylus Publishers, 2011)

Yes We Can! Improving Urban Schools through
Innovative Educational Reform
(Information Age Publishing, 2011)

African American Students in Urban Schools:
Critical Issues and Solutions for Achievement
(Peter Lang Publishing, 2012)

Black Males in Postsecondary Institutions:
Examining Their Experiences in Diverse
Institutional Contexts
(Information Age Publishing, 2012)

Black Male Teachers: Diversifying the United
States' Teacher Workforce
(Emerald Publishing, 2013)

An Educator's Guide to Working with African
American Students: Strategies for Promoting
Academic Success (2nd Edition),
(LEC Press, 2013)

Improving Urban Schools: Equity and Access in K-
12 STEM Education for All Students
(Information Age Publishing, 2013)

Teacher Education and Black Communities:
Implications for Access, Equity and Achievement
(Information Age Publishing, 2014)

African American Male Students in PreK-12
Schools: Informing Research, Policy and Practice
(Emerald Publishing, 2014)

*Autoethnography as a Lighthouse: Illuminating
Race, Research and the Politics of Schooling
(Information Age Publishing, 2015)*

*Priorities of the Professoriate: Engaging Multiple
Forms of Scholarship Across Rural and Urban
Institutions
(Information Age Publishing, 2015)*

*High School to College Transition Research Studies
(University Press of America, 2015)*

*Reaching the Mountaintop of the Academy:
Personal Narratives, Advice and Strategies from
Black Distinguished and Endowed Professors
(Information Age Publishing, 2015)*

*An Educator's Guide to Working with African
American Students: Strategies for Promoting
Academic Success (3rd Edition)
(LEC Press, 2016)*

*Black Female Teachers: Diversifying the United
States' Teacher Workforce
(Emerald Publishing, 2017)*

*Global Issues and Urban Schools: Strategies to
Effectively Teach Students in Urban Environments
around the World
(Information Age Publishing, 2019)*

*Community College Teacher Preparation for
Diverse Geographies: Implications for Access and
Equity to Preparing a Diverse Teacher Workforce
(Information Age Publishing, 2019)*

*The Dilemmas of Being an African American Male
in the New Millennium: Solutions for Life
Transformation (2nd Edition)*
(LEC Press, 2019)

*Conquering Academia: Transparent Experiences of
Diverse Female Doctoral Students
Information Age Publishing, 2019)*

*An Educator's Guide to Working with African
American Students: Strategies for Promoting
Academic Success (4th Edition)*
(LEC Press, 2019)

Order your books today at:
http://www.chancewlewis.com

About the Author

Dr. Chance W. Lewis is the Carol Grotnes Belk Distinguished Professor and Endowed Chair of Urban Education at the University of North Carolina at Charlotte. Additionally, Dr. Lewis is the Executive Director of the University of North Carolina at Charlotte's Urban Education Collaborative, which is publishing a new generation of research on improving urban schools.

Academic Background
Dr. Lewis received his B.S. and M.Ed. in Business Education and Education Administration from Southern University in Baton Rouge, Louisiana. Dr. Lewis completed his doctoral studies in Educational Leadership/Teacher Education from Colorado State University in Fort Collins, Colorado.

Teaching Background
Dr. Lewis currently teaches graduate courses in the field of urban education at the University of North

Carolina at Charlotte. His experiences span the range of K-12 and higher education. From 2006-2011, Dr. Lewis served as the Houston Endowed Chair and Associate Professor of Urban Education in the College of Education at Texas A&M University. Additionally, he was the co-director of the Center for Urban School Partnerships. In 2001-2006, he served as an assistant professor of teacher education at Colorado State University. From 1994-1998, Dr. Lewis served as a Business Education teacher in East Baton Rouge Parish Schools (Baton Rouge, LA), where he earned Teacher of the Year honors in 1997.

Research Background

Dr. Lewis has over 100 publications including 70+ refereed journal articles in some of the leading academic journals in the field of urban education. Additionally, he has received over $6 million in external research funds. To date, Dr. Lewis has authored/co-authored/co-edited over 22 books: *White Teachers/Diverse Classrooms: A Guide for Building Inclusive Schools, Eliminating Racism and Promoting High Expectations* (Stylus, 2006); *The Dilemmas of Being an African American Male in the New Millennium (Infinity, 2008); An Educator's Guide to Working with African American Students: Strategies for Promoting Academic Success* (Infinity, 2009); *Transforming Teacher Education: What Went Wrong with Teacher Training and How We Can Fix It* (Stylus, 2010); *White*

Teachers/Diverse classrooms: Creating Inclusive schools, Building on Students' Diversity and Providing True Educational Equity [2nd Ed.] (Stylus, 2011); *African Americans in Urban Schools: Critical Issues and Solutions for Achievement* (Peter Lang, 2012); *Yes We Can!: Improving Urban Schools through Innovative Educational Reform* (Information Age, 2011); *Black Males in Postsecondary Education: Examining their Experiences in Diverse Institutional Contexts* (Information Age, in press); *Black Male Teachers: Diversifying the United States' Teacher Workforce* (Emerald, 2013); *Improving Urban Schools: Equity and Access in K-12 STEM Education for All Students* (Information Age, 2013); *Black Male Teachers: Diversifying the United States' Teacher Workforce* (Emerald Publishing, 2013); and *An Educator's Guide to Working with African American Students: Strategies for Promoting Academic Success* [2nd Edition] (LEC Press, 2013); *African American Male Students in PreK-12 Contexts: Implications for Research, Policy & Practice (Emerald, 2014); Teacher Education & Black Communities: Implications for Access, Equity and Achievement* (Information Age, 2014); *Autoethnography as a Lighthouse: Illuminating Race, Research and the Politics of Schooling* (Information Age, 2015); *Priorities of the Professoriate: Engaging Multiple Forms of Scholarship across Rural and Urban Institutions* (Information Age, 2015); *High School to College*

Research Studies (University Press of America, 2015); *Reaching the Mountaintop of the Academy: Personal Narratives, Advice and Strategies from Black Distinguished and Endowed Professors* (Information Age, 2015); *An Educator's Guide to Working with African American Students: Strategies for Promoting Academic Success* [3rd Edition] (LEC Press, 2016], *Black Female Teachers: Diversifying the United States' Teacher Workforce* (Emerald, 2017); *Global Issues and Urban Schools: Strategies to Effectively Teach Students in Urban Environments* (Information Age, 2019); *Community College Teacher Preparation for Diverse Geographies: Implications for Access and Equity for Preparing a Diverse Teacher Workforce* (Information Age, 2019); *The Dilemmas of Being an African American Male in the New Millennium: Solutions for Life Transformation* [2nd Edition] (LEC Press, 2019); *Conquering Academia: Transparent Experiences of Diverse Female Doctoral Students* (Information Age, 2019) and *An Educator's Guide to Working with African American Students: Strategies for Promoting Academic Success* [4th Edition] (LEC Press, 2019).

Consulting Background

Dr. Lewis has provided consultative services (i.e., professional development and research services) to over 100 school districts and universities across the United States and Canada.

Contact Information

Dr. Lewis can be reached by e-mail at chance.lewis@gmail.com.

You can visit Dr. Lewis on the web at http://www.chancewlewis.com.

Preface

The Foundation for this Book!

There are certain times in history when certain books simply have to be written to address pertinent issues in society. Personally, *An Educator's Guide to Working with African American Students,* which is now in its fourth edition, is one of these books. Simply stated, I have implied answers to some pertinent questions in many of my other books (see earlier page for listing of books), articles and grant projects. However, as many times as I have tried to convince myself that I was not going to do the first, second and third editions of this book and even more the fourth edition (I really didn't want to do this one!) of this best-selling book since this issue seemed like 'common sense' in the field of education. Thankfully, I have come to realize that if I did not complete the various editions of this book, there would be a major void in the field of education, particularly as it pertains to classroom teachers who work directly with African American students.

An Educator's Guide to Working with African American Students continues to be very personal for me because I am deeply disappointed in a profession I love so much. To put it as plainly as I can, African American students are dying in the K-12 public, private and charter schools across our nation! While educators are quick to discuss a myriad of reasons why it is not their fault that African American students are not achieving, we (educators) never discuss what is in our locus of control when we have this population of students in our school districts, schools and classrooms. As a result, this book is a practical guide for K-12 educators to have as a valuable resource.

Webster (2019) defines the word guide as "something that provides a person with guiding information." As a result, I hope the fourth edition of this book reaches exactly the K-12 educators that it should reach to make a positive difference for African American students in the most affluent country in the world. I'm really tired of educators saying that nothing can be done for this group of students. My new motto is NO MORE EXCUSES. We can no longer, in this age of accountability, continue to see the achievement levels of this population of students and be comfortable with our work as professionals. As many educators in the research community note - the constant low achievement levels for African American students is known as Educational Malpractice.

Additionally, this book is for the African American students whose eyes I look into as I travel this great country. Their eyes look at me with all the potential that is trapped inside of them that is begging to be nurtured and developed fully. However, somehow or someway, their eagerness and excitement about school has been stripped from them and now they doubt if their educators truly believe they can achieve. I must say this to all educators - African American students want to learn, they want to perform well in school. Unfortunately, these students that are full of potential are then transformed into students full of frustration, self-doubt and underachievers because the very educators that, in most cases, are <u>paid</u> to educate these students are, in most cases, the same people that truly do not believe they can even perform academically. As a result, *some not all* educators view African American students as the main culprits who bring the standardized test scores of the school district and the school down without facing the fact that these students have not been educated in a way that excites them about learning.

Also, this book is for the parents who send their children to school expecting something great to happen for their children. This greatness that they expect is why many of them work one, two or three jobs to make sure their children have food on the table and a roof over their head just so they can make it to school. While many might not be the 'model parent' of what a school would want (i.e., a person who can volunteer all day, every day), they still are expecting greatness from teachers and the school for their children. However, when their child or children matriculate through our nation's schools, they are met with what I call "educational rhetoric."

This educational rhetoric tells the parent all that is perceived to be wrong with their child or children rather than what is needed to put your child in the best position to have a positive impact on their lives. I want you to know that I hear your voice as I write this book and I will let educators all across the nation know that you want your child/children to be prepared for what the future holds so they can reach their full potential.

Finally, I hear the voices, hopes and dreams of so many that have died for African American students to have a right to a quality education in this country. I often wonder what you think of the current conditions of education. Nevertheless, I thank you for making the ultimate sacrifice so that one day the education profession in this country can reach its full potential by serving the educational needs of African American students. I have come to learn that we have to continue to push until change happens. When this change happens, all of these African American students will have the opportunity to experience the 'good life' that only a quality education can provide.

I hope you enjoy the fourth edition of this book...let's take the journey!

-Chance W. Lewis, Ph.D.

Section I

The Role of the School Leader to Maximize the Learning Potential of African American Students

The mediocre teacher tells. The good teacher explains. The superior teacher demonstrates. The great teacher inspires.

William Arthur Ward

1

Leadership Matters: The Role of School Leaders in Ensuring African American Student Success

Attitude Reflects Leadership

Thousands of schools are currently low-performing in the United States, particularly those that serve African American students. That means that tens of thousands of students including African American students are not receiving a high-quality education. School Leaders let that sink in. How does this make you feel as a School Leader? I know for me it hurts my heart deeply because I think about the short-term and long-term implications for our most vulnerable children, their families and their communities. Additionally, this is important to me because I graduated from a low-performing school in Baton Rouge, Louisiana.

By all academic metrics, my high school was the worst high school in the city. Unfortunately, many of my classmates did not graduate, some were killed and others went to jail. On the other end of the spectrum, many of us did really well academically and have done many extraordinary things in society. So, I often wonder what could my school have done to meet the needs of all of the students? Why couldn't we be a high-achieving school like others in the city? We had a strong Principal who had a passion for the students and our school. Additionally, he constantly motivated us to do great things in life. I'm sure he carried the burden of us being a low-performing school but he believed in all of us because our school was 100% African American students. His most famous quote was, *"it's not your environment; it's you...you get to determine your future."* Years later, I think I now understand that he was telling us that despite the flaws of our school...we would need to overcome those so we can make something out of ourselves and be productive citizens.

I tell this story because even though I graduated from a low-performing urban school in a community that was struggling with many societal ills, it taught me everything I needed to know about low-performing schools that serve African American students. More specifically, I know what works and what does not work. I think it is even more important for you to know that I went back to my high school and did my student teaching internship and then started my teaching career at another high school in the city with very similar characteristics. Four years later, I was blessed to win Teacher of the Year honors. As a result, I have lived the low-performing school experience and have done fairly well. So, I know first-hand that successfully educating African American students is not only possible it should be the standard.

For this chapter, we will examine why *Leadership Matters* and key strategies School Leaders can implement to successfully lead schools with African American students. However, before we get to the strategies – we must be clear on who is really a School Leader. Additionally, we must look at the Heart, Will and Skill of School Leaders. If the School Leader does not have the Heart, Skill and Will all other strategies will not work for African American students to be able to excel academically.

Leadership Matters for African American Students

Leadership in schools is hard work! Additionally, leadership in schools that serve African American students and other students of color is an additional leadership task because these students have to interact daily with educators from other racial backgrounds who may or may not have preconceived stereotypes about their academic ability and you as a School Leader have to lead them in a way that successfully serves all students. Sometimes, School Leaders walk into this job with an uphill battle to change the school for the better. I want you to understand that you have to be prepared to change, rework, reimagine in transformative ways. It's not just academics; it's everything that impacts academics. This can include but not be limited to the following that have impact on academics and the accountability rating of the entire school:

- Aesthetics of the School;

- Hiring/Termination of Staff;

- Effective Building Operations;

- Transforming School Culture;

- Instructional Leadership;

- Growing Leaders;

- Before/After School Programming;

- Teacher Development;

- Academic Growth;

- Accountability/Testing;

- Effective Use of Funds (e.g., Title I, etc.);

- Parent Relationships/Involvement;

- Building & Sustaining Community Relationships;

- Leveraging Resources from the School District/Charter Organization;

- Fundraising;

- Many other duties...

At this point, we will not go into the details of each of these components but it is important to know that School Leaders must effectively deal with each of these components if they are going to raise the achievement levels of African American students and all other students in the school. While the burden of this tasks is huge in itself, it is important to know that it can be done and must be done to benefit the African American students that attend your school each and every day. Just remember, if I can attend a low-performing school and be successful in life, think about how many other youth can be successful if they attended a high-performing school.

We must remember that everything that we learn in this book is predicated on effective School Leadership because it impacts all facets of the learning process for African American students. The quote from my favorite movie, Remember the Titans, is as follows – *Attitude Reflects Leadership!* This means that how all the other stakeholders perform is based on leadership. So, think about this based on our quote, if teachers are teaching well it is because there is an expectation from leadership that they teach well. If they are teaching poorly, then the expectation of the School Leader allows this to happen and continue. If the school is low-performing, this means the leadership has to change the culture or change the game in all the areas listed earlier in this chapter to facilitate the desired change. This may involve changing people and/or leadership approaches for the academic performance of African American students to improve. This now brings us to a key question that we must consider. What leadership changes need to happen right now to unleash the full academic potential of African American students? Just remember, leadership matters!

> **Point to Ponder:**
>
> **What leadership changes need to happen to unleash the full academic potential of African American students?**

Who is a School Leader that best serves African American Students?

I feel it is important to clearly define what I mean by a School Leader that best serves African American students for this chapter. Many of you may believe I'm thinking of this in a traditional structure of Principal, Assistant Principal, Dean of Students, etc. However, for this book, I want us to re-envision the word School Leader. A School Leader is anyone in the building that has the Heart, Will and Skill despite their title to step up and step out of their current traditional role and serve in a leadership capacity whether large or small to make sure that the school is performing at peak performance levels for all students to succeed, including African American students. We must remember that this does not happen with a business as usual mindset. Something extraordinary must happen! As a result, who are all the people in the school that are willing to step up without even being assigned with a designated title of School Leader.

Activity

If you are ready to be a School Leader as I have defined above, here are the steps that you should immediately take:

- Inform your School Principal or Supervisor that you have decided that the status quo is no longer acceptable and you are willing to step to be a change agent;

- Let your School Principal or Supervisor know what role that you want to take on based on data, your observations of what is needed and your passion;

- Discuss your plan and timeline of how this will facilitate the development of the academic potential of all students including African American students.

Congratulations, you have taken the first step in the transformation process that will allow African American and all other students to be successful at your school/district. You are willing to put in the work to make it happen. Let's continue our journey. We must examine if the School Leader (regardless of title) has the Heart, Skill and Will to lead your school/district to be successful.

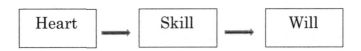

Characteristics of a School Leader that is Effective

<u>Examining the Heart of the School Leader</u>

If School Leaders are going to effectively serve African American students and all students in their school/district, it is critically important that we

8

examine their heart for this work. This is important because if they do not have the heart for serving African American students everything else does not matter. The heart has to be at the core because it is exhausting work because you must give so much of yourself. It is only the HEART that will allow you to continue when you are tired and ready to give up but you realize that you must continue if you are going to make a difference for African American students and other students in the school/district.

Litmus Test

To examine if the School Leader has a heart for this work, here is a litmus test that we can incorporate to check the heart. It is only a few questions but it will reveal their heart for this work. I provide the questions below and then we will look deeper into each of these questions:

- Do they enjoy working with African American students?

- Do they enjoy working in high-poverty schools?

- Do they have a heart for working in high-poverty communities?

- Do they firmly believe that the school can be successful?

9

Do they enjoy working with African American students?

This question is paramount. Given that the majority of schools in the United States have African American students, it is important this person wants to work with this population. What evidence have they shown that they have been effective with African American students? Given that we are in a data-driven profession they need to show proof they have made impact. Also, how do they engage with African American students? Do these students like them and give good reports about them? What evidence can they bring to the table to support that they enjoy working with African American students?

Do they enjoy working in high-poverty schools?

Unfortunately, all School Leaders do not like to work in all types of schools. Some people prefer to work in high-achieving, high-resourced, affluent suburban schools. However, it is important to note that many African American students are in high-poverty schools. As a result, we must ascertain if the School Leader wants to be in a school with the majority of students from high-poverty households. You should also ask the question if they think the income level in the household impacts intellectual ability. If they think it does, let them go now! Remember, you only want School Leaders that want to be at the school.

Do they have the heart to work in high-poverty communities?

Another key component in working with African American students is do they have the heart to engage in high-poverty communities where some African American students reside? We have to ensure that the School Leader has a heart to work and be present in these communities. I too often see School Leaders that only want to stay in the school building. However, schools are reflection of their communities. A key component of successfully working with African American students is to be present in their communities.

Do they firmly believe the school can be successful?

School Leaders must firmly believe that the school and students in the school can be successful. More specifically, if they do not believe in the school or the African American students, we do not want them as a School Leader. Of course, not many School Leaders will openly admit that they do not believe that a school will be able to be successful. I want you to watch their actions! Actions speaker louder than words! These actions will show if they truly believe school and African American students can be successful.

EXAMINING THE HEART OF THE SCHOOL LEADER

Given our focus on providing the best educational environment for African American students, it is important that we have concrete strategies for examining the heart of the School Leader. These three strategies will immediately provide the evidence needed to make a decision if these prospective School Leaders are ready for the responsibility to make sure African American students and all other students have the best learning environment. Please follow these in the order listed. Data about their performance should begin to illustrate if they will be effective in as little as a week from implementation.

STEP 1

Assign the prospective School Leader an area of leadership responsibility and evaluate them on the basis of their effectiveness of elevating all students, particularly African American students.

It is important at this stage that the prospective School Leader be assigned a smaller area of responsibility to evaluate their ability to successfully make sure African American students receive the proper support needed to reach their full academic potential. A few examples are as follows:

- *A certain group of teachers in a certain grade level have African American students that constantly score low on achievement tests. You determine instructional leadership is the answer. Assign the prospective School Leader to bring leadership to this situation and raise the achievement of these students. Evaluate how they handle this situation.*

- *Certain teachers are over-referring students for In-School Suspension (ISS) or Out-of-School Suspension (OSS) and you determine it is a classroom management issue. Evaluate how the prospective School Leader handles this situation.*

- *The school wants to increase the percentage of parents that are actively involved. Evaluate how the prospective School Leader handles that situation.*

STEP 2

Solicit feedback from African American students and other students about the School Leader's Heart for the Position

Once the prospective School Leader is provided with an area of responsibility, it is important to assess their heart for the job, their heart for the task assigned and their heart for the students. In my experience, I've learned students will tell you the truth both positively and negatively about people who work with them. It will be important to weigh the positive and negative comments/feedback to ascertain the students' perception about treatment for the work.

STEP 3

Evaluate their performance in leading student success particularly for African American students. Are the students making positive change academically?

In Step 3, this is where we evaluate the performance of the prospective School Leader on the tasks they were assigned to evaluate their heart for the job. At this final stage, one important question is the primary metric for evaluation. Did they successfully change the academic trajectory for African American students? Based on this question, can you clearly see that the situation is trending in the right direction? If the answer is NO, this clearly shows that they may not have the heart for working with African American students. Given that we are in a performance-based profession, we must have School Leaders that have heart for transforming the academic lives of all students, particularly African American students since this is the focus of this book.

EXAMINING THE SKILL OF THE SCHOOL LEADER

Now that we have examined the heart of the prospective School Leader, the next stage of this work is to examine their SKILL to do the job. Having the HEART for this work is only one component, they must have the SKILL to do the job as well. Without the SKILLS, the education organization will not successfully be effective for all the students, particularly African American students. As a result, let's explore the following topics for evaluate the skill of the School Leader that have direct impact on student success, particularly for African American students: (a) sustain and improve building operations; (b) evaluate the teaching performance of Instructional Staff; (c) School Transformation and Growth; (d) Reducing Discipline Issues; and (e) Family Engagement.

Sustain and Improve Building Operations

The first skill that a School Leader must have is the ability to sustain and improve building operations because it has a direct impact on student success. It is imperative they sustain what is going well and improve areas that are not working and impeding student achievement. This can range from the aesthetics of the building to classroom operation. As a result, the skills of a School Leader should be evaluated based on how well the person has shown a track record for improving operations or their ability to design key plans that will effectively make the necessary change needed in the school building. Here are three strategies:

- *Strategy 1. The School Leader should develop a 30, 60 and 90 day Implementation Plan that improves operations. The plan should be comprehensive that includes how current and future resources can be effectively utilized.*

- *Strategy 2. Develop a Campus Beautification Plan. After basic operations are handled then the School Leader must develop the campus to improve the look and appearance. Most low-performing schools that primarily serve African American students have dilapidated buildings and the aesthetics are not eye-appealing. This type of appearance of the school has psychological ramifications on students. It is important that they develop a short-term and long-term plan for campus beautification.*

- *Strategy 3. Partner with local businesses/sponsors that can help fund building improvements. For example, identify a playground that needs to be revitalized and partner with a local business and display that they are the official sponsor of the playground renovation project. School Leaders that have the SKILLS to make things happen will take this on because they realize all of this has impact on the success of all students including African American students.*

Evaluate the Teaching Performance of Instructional Staff

School Leaders must have the skill in evaluating the teaching performance of Instructional Staff. This skill is highly important because it has direct implications on the academic performance of African American students. Additionally, every School Leader has knowledge of Instructional Staff that are ineffective with African American students. As a result, it is of the utmost importance that these teachers are evaluated appropriately so solutions can be implemented for the betterment of the school. Here are three strategies for consideration:

- *Strategy 1. When evaluating Instructional Staff for effectiveness, don't focus on the teacher; focus on the students. Student interactions and dispositions tell you everything you need to know about the teacher.*

- *Strategy 2. When you find a member of your Instructional Staff that is ineffective, provide a clear professional growth plan to transform their classroom. Most Instructional Staff want to do well but don't know how.*

- *Strategy 3. For Instructional Staff that are effective with all students, including African American students, push them to go higher so they will not be comfortable at the current level. There is always room for improvement. Excellence has to be the standard!*

Reducing Discipline Issues

In the majority of schools, student discipline has reached a point where it is now impacting the teaching and learning process. This has resulted in African American students not reaching their full potential. I must note that in many cases, it is not even the fault of the students but the result of many things that have gone wrong in the school and classroom. In order to minimize student discipline issues and maximize academic growth, the following three strategies should be implemented:

- *Strategy 1. Instructional Staff must minimize discipline issues in the classroom through innovative instructional design that incorporates all five (5) senses throughout the class. The more interactive the class; the less discipline issues.*

- *Strategy 2. More teacher movement in the class which will facilitate teacher proximity in the classroom.*

- *Strategy 3. Incorporate Full-Class Restorative Circles. Restorative circles allow opportunities to think through past actions and improve future behavior.*

Family Engagement

The last skill that School Leaders must have is the ability to promote family engagement in the building. The family engagement component of School Leadership is absolutely essential. As a result, School Leaders must master this skill with innovative ideas to engage African American families in meaningful ways in the classroom. The three strategies are as follows:

- *Strategy 1. Incorporate neighborhood Block Parties to engage family in the attendance zone of the school. This works well at the beginning of the school year to allow families to meet the Instructional Staff and other school personnel.*

- *Strategy 2. Host Back-to-School Nights at a neutral location. Too often Back-To-School night or Curriculum Nights are at the school and only a small percentage of families*

19

attend. Change the location! Host it at a place that is fun and engaging for families!

- *Strategy 3. Have Instructional Staff develop specific ways for families to engage in the learning of their child(ren)! This can consist of parent involvement tasks that take 15-minutes or less to complete but are essential to the education of their child(ren). Additionally, it is important to note that all of these tasks do not have to be completed physically at the school. These tasks can be given out at one of your innovative events (see Step 1 and Step 2) and tell families that you will expect that they take care of these tasks. Watch how engagement increases!*

EXAMINING THE WILL OF THE SCHOOL LEADER

As we move towards the closure of this chapter, the third key aspect of a prospective or current School Leader must have is the WILL to make the school better for students, particularly African American students. For this book, the WILL that I am referring to is the ability to successfully lead and push the school to an entirely new level. Oftentimes, I see too much of what I call STATUS QUO leadership and it hurts African American students. By STATUS QUO Leadership, I mean many School Leaders are only satisfied with just getting through a school day or not rocking the boat. This type of School Leader unfortunately never raises the level of the instructional staff and ultimately African American students are usually hurt the worse by this inaction.

The School Leader that is needed for African American students and all students should be able to put a school on their back WILL them to the next level. They instill a belief through the entire school community that EXCELLENCE is the new normal. In other words, they do whatever they need to do to put a school community on their back and say we will transform our school for the benefit of all of our students with an intentional focus on our lowest-performing students – NO EXCUSES. These School Leaders incorporate the components discussed in this chapter and throughout this book to make sure it happens. Their VISION drives their PASSION.

FOR SCHOOL LEADERS THAT CARE

VISION DRIVES PASSION!!

Can you Navigate Bureaucracy?

The next sentence may or may not be a shocker to those of us in the field of education. Education organizations are a big bureaucracy. Similar to other organizations, there are webs of bureaucracy that must be successfully navigated if the School Leader will make the best learning environment for all students, particularly African American students. For clarity, here is an example of what I mean. A School Leader in a school district or charter organization knows that their instructional staff needs professional development in a specified area; however, the bureaucracy doesn't clearly provide instruction on how to receive the funds to fund these professional development activities. As a result, in the eyes of the School Leader, the bureaucracy only favors certain schools to get the necessary resources. Unfortunately, this leaves this School Leader on the 'outside looking in' when it comes to getting the resources they need for their school. This happens too often to School Leaders that are ready to make change. The bureaucracy is real!

The School Leaders that are able to successfully navigate the bureaucracy in such a way that moves their schools to benefit from the bureaucracy. They ask uncomfortable questions to figure out a way to get the resources. They find out who they need to meet to get the resources. They challenge the bureaucracy to be fair and equitable. In other words, they are not hesitant in letting the bureaucracy know when their school needs the necessary resources to get to the next level.

Can they grow leaders [current and aspiring] to benefit students?

Another critical component for School Leaders is to understand they can't do everything themselves. They understand they must grow leaders who can ultimately implement their vision for the benefit of all students, particularly African American students. I often say that great leaders can replicate themselves through other people. Given that schools are so demanding on the School Leader, the successful leaders develop, implement and evaluate their plans for growing current leaders. This is important because their growth is essential in making a difference for the students. One School Leader I was consulting with did not have a plan for her current leaders. It ultimately hurt this School Leader because the current School Leaders started to do their own thing and ultimately derailed the vision of the Principal. Once the Principal realized what they were doing, this person realized no plan was in place to grow the current leaders towards the vision.

Strategy: Develop and Implement a Strategy for Current Leaders

Additionally, School Leaders must also have a gift for evaluating future leaders and putting a plan in place to grow them. Here are a few questions to consider:

- Who among your current instructional staff has shown the leadership qualities as a teacher, counselor or social worker that has positively benefitted African American students?

- Who are your current staff members that are highly regarded among the staff?

- Who are those that are not currently in leadership that you can depend upon to make things happen at the school?

These qualities will allow you to identify future leaders that will assist you to successfully create an environment that will benefit all students, including African American students. Once they are identified, I find that the most effective way to get them on board is to personally invite them to be on your leadership team in whatever capacity you deem necessary. Personal invitations work best! They are even more effective when you also connect them with a plan of development for growth in the position. Remember, the successful School Leader is always looking for new talent to raise the level of the school to meet the needs of the students.

Conclusion

In closing, the first chapter of this book, *An Educator's Guide to Working with African American*

Students: Strategies for Promoting Success is to allow you the reader to understand that LEADERSHIP MATTERS in schools that serves all students, including African American students. Everything starts with leadership! Unfortunately, most schools that serve African American students have a leadership team in place that is ineffective in handling the full depth and breadth of the type of leadership that is necessary to make African American students successful. If this is not your school, great! Keep up the great work! If it is your school, we must continue to develop leaders that have the HEART, SKILL and WILL to serve African American students and other students that attend the school. Without these three components, the school will not be successful. I highly encourage you to incorporate strategies that I have provided throughout this chapter to make the school successful.

Experience teaches only the teachable!

Aldous Huxley

2

Professional Development that Works!

*Every moment of one's existence, one is growing
into more or retreating into less.*

Norman Mailer

School Leaders in this chapter, I want to walk you through professional development services that I have utilized with schools and school districts across the United States. I want you to understand that how you utilize your professional development budget has direct implications on how soon you can transform your school into a place of high academic achievement for all of your students, including African American students. Given that every state has over 500 schools that are given the accountability letter grade of D or F, it is imperative that you utilize your funding wisely to have maximum impact for students at your school. Let's examine what you can implement at your school:

No More Excuses:
School Transformation Program

The No More Excuses School Transformation Program is an in-depth, customized, school-specific program that addresses the real needs of the school to facilitate the School Transformation process.

Oftentimes, many School Leaders do not have a targeted plan for professional development. Usually, the professional development are on topics that do not necessarily move the needle in the academic performance of students on the school accountability ratings of the school or school district.

Whether you are looking to solve problems with cultural relevance in the classroom, parental involvement, student leadership or anything in the classroom...I'm more than able to diagnose and work out a customized plan that will put your school or school district on the right path for sustainable success. Let's examine a few of the most requested professional development services that have proven success across the United States.

No More Excuses:
Culturally Relevant Teaching Strategies that Improve Academic Achievement

This series of professional development provides School Leaders and all of their educators with a clear path on how to implement culturally relevant teaching into the classroom. Unfortunately, many teachers have heard of Culturally Relevant Teaching (CRT) but very few actually know how to implement in their classrooms. This factor alone is one of the primary reasons we often see high discipline issues, low teacher and student enthusiasm and substandard academic performance on standardized tests. As a result, we will continue to see the accountability ratings of D or F for schools around the country.

In this Culturally Relevant Teaching (CRT) Professional Development Series, I will show your faculty, staff and administrators:

- How to find and understand current trends and fads that your students are paying attention to (this alone will help your teachers connect more deeply with their students);

- How to incorporate these concepts into the lesson plans in a way that not only engages their students, but satisfies curriculum and teaching requirements;

- How to create their lessons in a way that feels authentic...NOT like they're trying to "bribe" their students' engagement with fun concepts.

More specifically, your staff will be thoroughly trained in Culturally Relevant Teaching and they will start the process of building a database of effective lessons that will include Culturally Relevant lesson plans by grade level, content area and academic standard. This will be sustainable over time as educators change in your school building. Additionally, it will provide benefit to all of your instructional staff by actually showing them step-by-step logistics in creating Culturally Relevant lesson plans.

No More Excuses:
Strategies for High Achievement of Boys of Color

This series of professional development provides School Leaders and all of their educators with effective strategies for working with Boys of Color. Unfortunately, in most schools, teachers have had the toughest time in connecting with Boys of Color. As a result, this professional development series provides proven strategies of what teachers can do to engage this population. Usually, I hear language such as the following: "I don't know what's going on with these boys. We can't reach them and they're just becoming problem students." Sound familiar? Many schools struggle to connect with boys of color and engage them in learning – and boys of color are almost always the population that leads low performance. In this professional development series, I will show your staff:

- How to truly understand the motivations of the boys in their classrooms – and understand what makes them act in a certain way in specific situations...

- How to appropriately teach the boys in their classroom while also ensuring they don't ignore the girls...

- How to use boys' natural personalities and predispositions as a teaching aid, rather than attempting to overcome them with stricter rules and punishments.

This professional development series will have an immediate impact on the performance of level of all Boys of Color in your school or school district. Additionally, this professional development series will also address the struggle that many educators have with Boys of Color in their classrooms. As a result, the benefit for your school or school district is key to the overall success.

No More Excuses:
Strategies for Increasing Parent Involvement Now!

It's no secret that the more parents are involved, the more successful a school is. Whether it's PTA meetings, parent classroom helpers, or opening the lines of communication between parent and teacher...parent involvement is directly related to the success of your school. But it's not always that easy to get parents involved and connected. Until now, in this professional development series, I will show your staff the following:

- The true effect that parental involvement has on each students' ability to achieve success...

- How to prepare for parental involvement – so when it does happen...your teachers are ready to capitalize on it the right way...

- Strategies to implement right away that will increase parent involvement (in one school, my strategy increased parent involvement by over 60% after just ONE event)...

By implementing this professional development series, your school or district will be on a pathway for true parental involvement. We cannot continue to underestimate how little our staff knows about strategies to truly engage parents. Many parents want to be involved but they haven't been given the right types of opportunities to be involved. We must remember that many parents had bad experiences in school so to change their perception, we have to be proactive in getting them involved in the school.

Conclusion

School Leaders as we close out this chapter, it is very important to remember that your professional development must be transformational. We can no longer just allow anyone to come into our school buildings and provide professional development that does not immediately move the needle in progress for our schools. If true school transformation is going to happen, we need to have serious discussions with professional development service providers on what educators will be able to do 'starting tomorrow' after the training. This is critical because if they [educators] are not immediately able to implement what they learning in a training, the money paid to consultants has been wasted and the return on investment will be minimal. As a result, I encourage all school leaders to only allow professional development that moves forward school transformation. If I can ever be of service, please do not hesitate to contact me at chance.lewis@gmail.com or visit my website at http://www.chancewlewis.com.

Section II

The Role of the Teachers and Instructional Staff to Maximize the Learning Potential of African American Students

3

An Educator's Self-Reflection on Teaching African American Students

"Self-Reflection allows you to find the truth within you"
-Author unknown

Self-reflection in any profession, particularly education, is especially important. This allows each of us to examine the impact that we are making in our individual lives, in our local communities and in the world around us. However, in the field of education, it is my personal opinion that educators, especially classroom teachers who have a primary responsibility for educating our nation's youth, do not take enough time to truly self-reflect on the impact they are making through their work; their communities, but most of all in their students' lives. As a result of this growing trend in the field of education, I want to explore four critical areas all educators, especially classroom teachers, should consider starting their individual self-reflection with the following questions:

(1) Why did you choose to enter the field of education?

(2) Are you afraid of your African American students?

(3) Do you really believe your African American students can achieve academically?

(4) How are your African American students benefiting from having you as an educator?

Why Did You Choose the Teaching Profession?

As we venture this journey of self-reflection, which I feel is critically important for educational professionals, particularly teachers, the first question you have to continually ask yourself is, "why did I choose the teaching profession?" This question is the foundation of your work and a question you must understand and embrace if you are going to successfully work with African American students. Hopefully, as you reflect and ponder your answer to this question, you chose this profession because you honestly believe that all students, including African American students, can learn at a high level, achieve high academic outcomes and become better citizens in our great nation as a result of your efforts as an educator. As we reflect back to the time that many of us started in this profession, we really believed we could change the world and that our students would be a beacon of hope in our world. However, in some strange way, a variety of internal and external factors have caused many educators to change their viewpoints about the learning capabilities of many African American children.

Unfortunately, we have surpassed the point when many teachers, counselors, administrators and other educators have prematurely (in their minds) failed African American students before they even start their academic school years or critically engaged academically in their schools at the academic year. *Whether it is based on rumors or societal stereotypes we have heard about the students (probably in the teacher's lounge) from other educators or our own individual stereotypical beliefs about an African American student's ability based solely upon their outer appearance, all come together inside of the academic setting.* Most often, this has a detrimental impact on the African American student's self-esteem and their perceptions of what they are able to accomplish in the classroom.

As I travel around the country working with different schools and school districts, I strongly try to portray the message, "don't judge the book by its cover." To translate this into academic terms, don't look at the student's academic record or listen to other's perceptions about the student's ability before they come into your classroom. The reason for this is that this student may have overcome a huge personal obstacle and completely turned their life around. Another reason is that this student may have crossed paths with a "bad teacher or an unmotivated teacher" (there are still many of these teachers floating the education world) that pushed them to negatively perform in the school setting. Basically, what I am saying is to give the African American student, or any student for that matter, a fair chance to be successful in your classroom.

Now, I return to my original question, why did you choose to enter the teaching profession? My hope is that you had that wonderful fire burning inside of you because you wanted to see "ALL" students achieve, particularly African American students. Remember, it may be YOU, not someone else, who will possibly change this child's life forever. So, I ask in the most heartfelt way possible through the power of the words on this paper, to recapture the passion that led you to choose education as a career.

Are You Scared of your African American Students?

Before we can get into an in-depth discussion about how to work with African American students, I must first ask you a straightforward question. Are you scared of your African American students? If your answer is "yes" or "maybe yes," we first must address this problem. One thing I do need you to know is that *YOU CANNOT TEACH ANY CHILD THAT YOU ARE SCARED OF!* This is a fundamental fact. If you are scared of your African American students, particularly your African American males, one of two things will eventually happen.

> You Can't Teach Any Child That You Are Scared Of!

First, they will become total disruptions in the classroom and you will become so frustrated that you will get to a point where you do not want to enter the classroom because you know there is a potential for a confrontation with this student every day. Second, there is a potential, through your frustration, that you will overexert your power as a teacher and try to get these students removed from your class in any way possible. For example, the odds greatly increase that you will consider and act upon referring these students for special education testing even though you honestly know nothing is wrong with the African American student, it is just that you have lost control of the classroom.

Another example is that you will repeatedly send African American students to the principal's office to have out-of-school or in-school suspension although the offenses committed were, at best, minor offenses. Even worst, we then tell other teachers and educators (in the hallway or the teacher's lounge) how horrible these students are when the root of the problem is that you are scared of your students.

> Most African American students are
> suspended and lose academic learning time
> because the teacher has lost control of the
> classroom!

Lisa Delpit (1995) documented that there are three types of White teachers that work with African American students: (a) those White teachers that are scared of all Black students; (b) those White teachers that are scared of some Black students; and (c) those White teachers that are not scared of Black students. Which type of teacher are you? It is my belief that these three points are true for teachers of all racial backgrounds.

For those teachers who are honestly not scared of their students, these teachers have been found to have African American students who achieve at high levels academically. To be honest, the way that you show a student you care is by providing examples and making them act appropriately. This is why when we examine the educational landscape of successful schools and take a peek inside the classrooms of effective teachers, these teachers are not scared of their African American students. Instead, these effective teachers push this student population behave accordingly and push them do their work at a high level. Also, this type of approach works when guests are in the classroom. By this I mean these effective teachers can give all students in their class what I call a "teacher look" and they will immediately straighten up and get refocused on their coursework. An example of a "teacher look" I had when I was growing up was when my grandmother would give me a look, often from the choir stand in our church, when I was acting up with my friends. I immediately knew at that point that I had better get it together or there would be serious consequences.

As a result, teachers I am asking that you get over any fears that you have and take control of your class. This is not done in a way that is damaging to your students but in a way that is commonly referred to as discipline with love. Please remember, *YOU CANNOT TEACH ANY STUDENT IF YOU ARE SCARED OF THEM! WE MUST GET OVER OUR FEARS AND MAKE A POSITIVE IMPACT ON OUR STUDENTS' LIVES.*

Are you planting seeds of greatness into your students?

As educators teaching 21st century or millennial students, we must ask ourselves the critical questions concerning what are we planting into our students. The reason I pose the question is that often African American students are leaving school with nothing indicating that they spent years in our schools. That is, no education, no tangible skills to advance in society, no social skills, no academic skills, no job skills, just nothing. While we as educators are quick to point the finger (and understandably so) at a variety of factors including, but not limited to: (a) parents; (b) the communities and their resulting support systems where African American students reside; (c) family socioeconomic standing; and (d) family educational background, we must remember all of these characteristics do not tell the entire story. Unfortunately, we never point the finger at ourselves to truly examine our role in the miseducation and the lack of preparation for the 'real-world' for these African American students (Woodson, 1903).

In many classrooms across the United States, we can walk in and find that teachers are giving everything they can to their students. These teachers provide solid academic content, culturally relevant pedagogy and an excitement for the teaching and learning process. These are the teachers that, through their daily efforts, are preparing African American students to fulfill all the great potential they have inside.

Further, these teachers educate all students, including African American students, despite the aforementioned circumstances. They honestly understand that if true change will be made for African American students, they will have to be change agents in their lives. The reason they have to be change agents in the lives of these students is that they understand that they may be one of few adults in the lives of their African American students that the student can depend on for solid academic preparation. Additionally, these teachers serve as a role model of the characteristics they need to be successful in their life aspirations. As a result, they know that not only are they preparing their students to successfully complete an academic course to meet some arbitrary state education requirement, but they are preparing students to use the academic content as a necessary tool for survival in the 'real world.' Through it all, these are the teachers that African American students remember as the educators who took the time to shape them for where they are going in life. These types of teachers are vitally important to have in all of our schools if academic achievement is going to happen on a consistent basis.

Unfortunately for African American students, only a small percentage of teachers have this type of 'liberatory' mindset towards their life's outlook. In many schools across the United States, we still have teachers who look at their positions as just a job or something that they chose to do because they couldn't do anything else. They only see their students as people they need to watch for the duration of a particular academic semester or year. Even further, some teachers view their African

American students as a menace to society and talk about this group of students badly with their co-workers, administrators and even their family members.

In other examples, some teachers often allow African American students to do nothing in the classroom or anything they want to do that is counterproductive to improving their academic ability in the classroom. I know this may sound like an oxymoron, but let me explain what I mean. For example, when some teachers allow African American students to do nothing or anything that want in the classroom, they allow these students to sit in their classrooms and not turn in any academic work at all. If they turn in their work, it is so mediocre that the students know that they do not have to push hard to meet teacher expectations. These teachers often just tell these students that if they remain quiet they can stay in the classroom. This is academic and life suicide for the African American student. This type of teaching practice cannot continue to occur in our schools. If it does, our schools become the factory of mediocre students.

> Telling an African American student to sit in the classroom and be quiet without having expectations for them to complete any work is academic suicide.

On the other end of the spectrum, some teachers allow their African American students to do anything they want in the classroom that is non-academic. By this I mean, African American students are allowed to play non-academic games (i.e., dominoes, card games, dice, etc.), watch non-academic videos, surf the Internet to catch up on the latest sports scores, soap operas or browse on various Internet and social media sites that are not blocked by their respective school districts. Some in the educational community will say this is the equivalent of doing nothing; however, in my opinion this is the teacher who allows the African American student to do anything in the classroom as long as they do not bother the teacher or interrupt class during that class session.

In closing this chapter, I am asking or even begging teachers to take a self-reflection of why they entered the great profession of education in the first place. The answer to their question is critical before we can move on to any other subject that I intend to address in this book. The way you, a state-certified educator, charged with enhancing the life opportunities for students, answer this question, is in direct correlation to your success in working with African American students. We, as educators, must remember that African American students are not some group of students who came into your classrooms not wanting to achieve...they are looking for educators that will provide the actual structure inside the classroom to facilitate their academic potential. As the ever-popular verse from the Holy Bible notes, "you reap what you sow."

Further, Jawanzaa Kunjufu (2001) asserted that African American students believe the following:

> *I don't become what I think I can;*
>
> *I don't become what you think I can;*
>
> *I become what I think you think I can!*

Given this quote, what do you really believe about the academic potential of your African American students? What you believe will eventually be revealed in the academic setting. As I close this chapter, I wonder if we (administrators, teachers, counselors, etc.) would educate African American students differently if they were our own biological children. Just a thought!

4

Connecting with your African American Students in the Academic Setting

Kids don't remember what you try to teach them. They remember what you are.

Jim Henson

During the past twenty years since the release and widespread dissemination of the groundbreaking *A Nation at Risk* (1983) report, the education profession has made great strides toward increasing the academic rigor of our nation's public schools. This increased attention on academic rigor and revised state content standards has resulted in curricular transformation, with increased emphasis in the Science, Technology, Engineering and Mathematics (STEM) fields with the hopes of keeping the United States competitive with other nations. A more recent example is the passing of the *Race to the Top* and the *Every Student Succeeds* legislation, which was part of the American Recovery and Reinvestment Act of 2009. President Barack Obama and United States Secretary of Education Arne Duncan announced this legislation on July 24, 2009. This new iteration of the previous No Child Left Behind Act of 2002 awarded millions of taxpayer dollars to states for satisfying certain educational policies, such as performance-based standards (often referred to as an Annual professional performance review) for teachers and principals, complying with nationwide standards, promoting charter schools, and computerization (Wikipedia, 2012). This sweeping legislation has changed the landscape of schools by focusing an increased emphasis on standardized testing, accountability and educational entrepreneurship with a focus on charter schools.

However, when I examine all of the academic barometers, the African American student is still at or near the bottom of every indicator that focuses on positive academic achievement. This makes me ask, what has gone wrong in the educational system of the United States in relation to supporting these students? Is this an unintended consequence of the *Brown vs. Board of Education* of Topeka, Kansas (1954) decision? How is it that African American students are not reaching or exceeding the same academic levels as their counterparts? How has this issue become so widespread that the majority of schools and school districts across the country are seeking answers how to work effectively with this population of students? Has the education profession lost faith in this group of students? Why do many educators believe this population is the sole reason that their school is not making Adequate Yearly Progress (AYP), which is an indicator that public schools must meet on annual basis?

My own personal thoughts and my experiences in schools continue to inform me that it is not because African American students are academically inferior, do not want to achieve or hate school. The basic reason they are not achieving is because their teachers and other educational professionals have not made a conscious effort to 'connect' with them in the academic setting. We must remember that these students are the descendants of such great thinkers that produced the pyramids in Africa, built Washington, D.C., our nation's capital, performed the first open heart surgery, along with many other accomplishments.

It comes down to this, until teachers and other educational professionals learn to reach the African American students in the classroom, we will continue to see the same educational attainment rates and outcomes of this population despite the widespread reform efforts. As a result, I want to explore the notion of 'connection' and why it is so important in the educational setting.

Strategies for Connecting with African American Students

To provide a foundation for this section, let us examine the following definitions of the root word of connection, which is the word *connect*. According to Webster (2009), the root word *connect* is defined as: (a) to have or become joined; (b) to have or establish a rapport; (c) to establish connections; (d) to join or foster together through intervening; and (e) to place or establish in a relationship. In translating each of these definitions into an academic context, we learn that someone (the educator) has to be joined with someone else (the African American student) in a meaningful way in order for learning to occur in the academic setting.

As we delve further into the idea of connection with the African American student, we must understand why this is critically important in the classroom. In my mind, this concept is important for the following reasons: (1) when rapport (see definition listed previously) is established with the African American student, the student will know they can trust you as an adult and as an educator with their academic lives; (2) connection is more than academics, it is for life; (3) when true connection is made the African American student will not want to disappoint you; (4) connection is when the African American student can look at you as a role model, a first step; (5) connection is one of the main ingredients for students to perform better on standardized tests; (6) connection makes students want to study because they do not want to disappoint their teacher; and (7) connection makes students want to explore the concept of extending their educational pursuits beyond the K-12 setting to postsecondary and career options

Educators, as you review this list, I hope it is clear just how important *connecting* with your students can be. We must now move to the very basic things necessary to establish this connection in your classroom or your school. However, before we do, let me reiterate, in a visual format, the reasons why it is so critically important to connect with your African American students.

Connection and positive relationships between teachers and African American students are absolutely necessary for academic achievement!

Table 1: Important Reasons to Connect with African American Students

Important Reasons to 'Connect' with African American Students
1. When rapport (see definition listed previously) is established with the African American student, they know they can trust you as an adult and as an educator.
2. Connection is more than academics, it is for life.
3. When true connection is made with the African American student they will not want to disappoint you.
4. Connection is when the African American student can look at you as a role model.
5. Connection is one of the main ingredients for students to perform better on standardized tests.
6. Connection makes students want to study.
7. Connection makes students want to explore the concept of extending their educational pursuits beyond the K-12 setting.

How Do I Connect with African American students?

As I have traveled the country providing professional development sessions for various schools and school districts, speaking at conferences and/or having informal conversations with educators, many of these educators who have excellent academic credentials mention they cannot master the art of connecting with students in their schools and/or districts. The underlying truth is many educators want to connect, they just do not know how to do it. This is why I am really frustrated with so many prolific scholars and research organizations, including universities, because we (the researchers and the scholarly community) never tell educators how to connect with their students, particularly African American students. As a result, in this section of the chapter, I want to provide some answers to this question as it relates to connecting with African American students.

First, I would encourage everyone to read a powerful chapter by a leading scholar who has done more than her part to provide answers to educators. Dr. Gloria Ladson-Billings at the University of Wisconsin-Madison wrote a groundbreaking chapter in my previous book, *White Teachers/Diverse Classrooms: A Guide for Building Inclusive Schools, Promoting High Expectations and Eliminating Racism* (2011) entitled, "Culturally Relevant Pedagogy: How Do

We Do It?" I would encourage any educator that is interested to pick up a copy of this book and read this chapter. This chapter really breaks down, in simplistic terms, one of the educational buzzwords, "Culturally Relevant Pedagogy" so the educators who truly have a passion to make a true connection with any student can use this concept in their classroom. This chapter is a must-read if you truly want to make a connection.

Second, as an educator, you will have to understand the African American student's world. By this I mean, we have to change the mindset of having to 'fix' students so they can be successful in school. This is a deficit model of thinking that has greatly impacted the academic achievement of so many African American students. As a result, we need to really investigate and find out what our students' value (not assume) and find ways to incorporate their world into our classroom and in our curriculum to improve their educational achievement levels and improve their life opportunities. When we (educators) find out what African American students' value, we can use this knowledge to bring relevancy to our lessons. It is unfortunate that in the 21st century, students in our classrooms are still asking one of the oldest questions in the field of education, "Why do I have to do this?" Also, a new question is also paramount, 'how do I see my life inside the curriculum?' It is critically important we understand that relevancy is necessary.

I firmly believe that teachers and all other educators in our nation's schools must be able to see culturally relevant lessons that still meet academic standards but really pique the interest of 21st century African American students. There are academic lessons that we can teach in all academic content areas on McDonald's, Hip-Hop music, sports, current events, the arts, urban clothing, etc. However, we have to be willing to see academic lessons inside of what the African American students enjoy and take advantage of teachable moments. This is the main way we can 'connect' with African American students and raise their academic achievement levels. We (educators) must remember that mastering the concepts for a particular content area (mathematics, reading, science, etc.) is the same; the problem is that we do not provide cultural relevancy for all students. I would also encourage educators to study the work of Jawanza Kunjufu. I greatly admire his work because he provides strategies for educators to reach African American students.

Finally, to make a connection with African American students, we must obtain new excitement about your lesson planning and teaching techniques. Unfortunately, I continue to observe too many educators who are not excited about teaching students, particularly African American students. More specifically, many of these educators do not want to be in their current positions. As a result,

African American students are much less likely to be excited about coming to school and excelling academically if the people who are responsible for their education are not excited about their work.

> To make a connection with African American students, we must obtain new excitement about your lesson planning and teaching techniques.

In the 21st century, we need educators who are excited about the educational process despite the bureaucracy and the politics of education. We must understand that African American students, just like all students, take on some of the character traits of their educators. If this is the case, what does that say about you as an educator? If your students are not achieving academically, what role did you play in this? Educators, we must understand that a major part of connecting with students is first showing them that you genuinely care! Remember, you cannot fake caring for your students! If you fake it…your students will know instantly!

What is the Benefit for me as an Educator?

As we continue on this journey, we must understand that the benefits of connection are not just for African American students, but it can also be for the teacher. It is safe to say that the majority of teachers in the United States, particularly in urban educational settings, want to connect and build a professional relationship with their students. Building a connection with your African American students in ways that I have laid out in this chapter will bring you great joy in this profession. We must understand that as teachers seek to build connection with their students a few things must happen in the process. I will attempt to list a few of these benefits in Table 2.

[see next page for Table 2]

Table 2: The Benefits of Connecting with African American Students

The Benefits of Connecting with African American Students
1. Your African American students will become more academically engaged.
2. Your African American students will attempt to go above your expectations.
3. African American students will have an increased excitement about your class.
4. African American students will not want to disappoint you and ruin the connection that has been built.
5. Discipline issues will decline dramatically as a result of the connection.
6. Academic test scores of your African American students will improve.
7. African American students will not waste valuable time in your classroom.

Educators, as we reflect on the aforementioned list in Table 2, many would love to say that they demonstrate these characteristics in the classroom on a consistent basis. So, what is preventing us from having solid academic achievement for African American students? Educators may ask, "How can I have the ideal African American student(s) that I can reach and it doesn't feel like such a great barrier to reach them?" I can practically hear you talking through the pages of this book!

To benefit from the connection with your students, you must do the following:

[see next page for Table 3]

Table 3: Benefits of Connecting with African American Students

Benefits of Connecting with African American Students
1. You need to genuinely care about the well-being of all of your students, particularly your African American students.
2. You must look at your teaching as a matter of life and death because for many of your African American students this is the case.
3. You must be willing to go into your African American students' neighborhoods to save them.
4. You have to do your homework and prepare quality lessons if you want your African American students to do their homework.
5. You can't expect African American students to achieve if you don't have high expectations.
6. You must TEACH them.

As a result, I will briefly elaborate on each of these.

You need to genuinely care about the well-being of all of your students, particularly your African American students.

As I stated earlier in this chapter, caring is the first essential ingredient you must have if connection is going to be made. I am so disappointed in many educators who blame African American students *for everything* when many of the problems can be solved by simply caring for these students. We must clearly understand that many of your African American students are more concerned about your level of caring for them versus your academic credentials or the academic standards you are trying to teach them. Not to say that your academic credentials are not important, but *most* important is the notion of caring for African American students.

You must look at your teaching as urgent to the life and death of students because for many of your African American students this is the case.

Educators, we must understand that for many African American students, educational attainment is their only legal way to a better life in the United States. Far too many of our nation's students, particularly African American students, face situations that no kid should have to deal with. Consequentially, if we are going to change the future, we are going to have to prepare them today. We need to approach our teaching, our lesson planning, our curricular materials, our schools, our educational policies and all other activities from a life or death viewpoint. If not, we will continue to see the current trend of African American students falling through the cracks of our educational system.

You must be willing to go into your African American students' neighborhoods to save them.

Educators, the time has run out for us just showing up at the school site unmotivated and then going home. We need educators who have such an interest in their students that when their students, African American students in particular, are absent for long periods of time they will take it upon themselves to begin to investigate what is going in the student's life. Sometimes the teacher has to go and find the students. Now, I know that many educators may say that this task is not in their job description. Connection with your students, particularly African American students, may have you doing many different tasks that are not in your job description like sitting in a courtroom with these students, etc. Nevertheless, to say it as plainly as I can, we must be able to go into their neighborhoods, if need be, to save them.

You have to do your homework and prepare quality lessons if you want your African American students to do their homework.

Educators, specifically teachers, we must get back to the craft of taking the necessary time to adequately prepare culturally relevant lessons for our students. Oftentimes, many teachers just teach from the same lessons plans year after year without any adaptation. As fast as the world is changing, we can no longer prepare all students, particularly African American students, from outdated and irrelevant lesson plans that have no connection to their everyday lives.

You can't expect African American students to achieve if you don't have high expectations.

Educators, one thing that continues to bother me is how we continue to allow African American students to perform at substandard levels and not address this with them in the classroom. We allow them to turn in mediocre work, come to class late and basically get away with everything. This is not how the real world works. African American students have to know that in your classroom they have to put forth their best effort in all areas. Remember, your students, particularly African American students, will only perform as high as you expect them to. So, I ask, do you really think African American students can perform at a high level academically?

In conclusion, I have tried to lay out for you the numerous benefits of connection in classrooms across the United States to assist African American students in reaching their potential. I have provided evidence of why connecting is important, strategies for connecting with your students, the benefits for connecting with your students, explaining how to connect with your students, the benefits of connecting for educators with steps to reap benefits. I hope these words will travel through the halls of our nation's schools and reach those educators that truly want to make a positive connection with their African American students.

The bottom line is results; anything else

is rhetoric! – Dr. Lee Jones

5

Classroom Management and African American Students

Teachers who have the best managed classrooms are those who spend the first two weeks of class teaching and practicing their procedures and routines.

Michael Mills

Educators, as you read and reflect on the contents of this book, I know this specific chapter is one that is of great interest to each of you given the focus on classroom management. As I travel around the world, many teachers and other educators constantly ask the question: *How do I reach the students of this generation and handle classroom management, particularly for African American students?* Even further, how do I reach my African American students and have them sit down and focus long enough for me to deliver a quality lesson?

I have come to understand that the issue of classroom management is the number one issue for over 90 percent of the K-12 teaching force in the United States. More important, for new teachers (years 0-5), this is the main issue directly affecting whether they stay or leave the profession. According to the education research literature, this is probably the most studied topic, with a plethora of journal articles and books; however, all of this research has not made it to the practitioner at the grass root level to handle the day-to-day management issues in the nation's classrooms.

As a result, in this chapter, I will discuss some basic concepts that all educators should understand and be able to implement to improve classroom management issues on a daily basis. More specifically, I will cover the following general topics: (1) classroom management expectations at your school site; (2) classroom management expectations in your classroom; (3) Discipline from a Distance (Involving Key Family Members); (4) Teacher Proximity; (e) The Teacher Look; and (f) Classroom Arrangement.

Classroom Management Expectations at Your School Site

Educators, as we explore this issue of classroom management, we must understand it from two perspectives: (1) the school district level and (2) the school level. These two perspectives are important since these two entities implement the guiding policies regarding classroom management. As a result, teachers, counselors, social workers, teacher aides, coaches, bus drivers, etc. cannot do anything pertaining to classroom management outside the boundaries of the district and school policies related to this issue. So before we move on, I must offer suggestions that assist us in understanding classroom management issues at the policy level.

First, I am encouraging every educator to read their respective school/district manual which outlines the policies as related to classroom management. While for many educators this may be boring reading material, this is critical because you must understand the school district and the school building position on classroom management because this is the primary policy that impacts African American students disproportionately in an unfavorable way. So, please take time to read this information carefully.

Second, after you have obtained this new knowledge, you should begin to ask questions to your building principal about the components of this policy that appear to be vague. This is important because if something is subject to your interpretation, you need to know the viewpoint of your principal. By knowing the position of your building principal on a particular issue, you will have the necessary knowledge should something happen in your classroom. This will also assist you in garnering support from your principal in different classroom situations.

Third, after you have read the district and school policies on classroom management, I want you to begin to envision how you can conceptualize a plan for dealing with this in your classroom. We must understand that this requires a thinking process that fits your personality traits. While you have seen many classroom management strategies from other teachers during your time as a student, the one I found that works best is one that fits your individual personality. Given this, I now want to move into the topic of classroom management expectations in your classroom.

Classroom Management Expectations in Your Classroom

Now that we have an understanding of the various policies governing classroom management and discipline procedures in the school district, we are ready to implement our plans for the expectations of students regarding management and discipline issues in our classroom. As previously mentioned, this is something that should be well thought out before students start the academic school year. So, as we take this journey to tackle the classroom management issue, let's discuss several phases that I feel are important: (1) pre-planning for management in your classroom; (2) the first day of school; (3) consistency in management; and (4) handling unexpected issues during the year.

Pre-Planning for Classroom Management

To have an effective classroom, it is critically important that you pre-plan for classroom management. This allows you to provide the framework for how students will behave in your classroom. To do so, I am providing several key questions that you must ask yourself as you begin the pre-planning process.

Table 1: Key Questions for Pre-Planning of Classroom Management

Key Questions for Pre-Planning of Classroom Management
1. What should happen when students enter your class?
2. What happens if students are late for no valid reason?
3. What is your policy on minor classroom disruptions?
4. What is your policy on major classroom disruptions?
5. What is your policy on students sleeping in class?
6. What is your policy on homework that is turned in late with no approved excuse?
7. What is your policy on students leaving class to go to the restroom?
8. What is your policy on electronic devices (i.e., smartphones, iPads, etc.) that are brought into the classroom?
9. What is your policy if you catch a student cheating on an assignment or test?
10. What is your policy if a student refuses to do their work in your classroom?

While this list of questions may not be exhaustive of every situation, it can be used as a guide to begin the pre-planning process for management. I would really encourage each teacher reading this book to honestly answer each one of these questions. By doing so, you can begin to build a framework for how management will be handled in your classroom.

We must understand that having a classroom management plan does not mean that you are ready to punish students for every little act they commit; you are just providing a plan to teach students how they should behave in your classroom. Given this, you should now begin to write your classroom management plan.

Writing Your Classroom Management Plan

As we begin the process of writing your classroom management plan, I want you to understand that this document should be clear and succinct so anyone can understand how management and discipline issues will be handled in your classroom. Also, this should outline other classroom procedures as well. However, this document should not be so lengthy that no one will read it. I would recommend that your classroom management plan be no longer than three (3) typed pages. This will give students, parents and administrators the opportunity to read through a document that is clear but not too lengthy.

The first item I feel you need to include in your management plan is your contact information that you feel comfortable releasing to the public. This should include items such as your name, phone numbers you would like students and parents to have, a valid e-mail address, hours available for parent conferences, and your professional website (I highly encourage a website). Providing this information shows that you are inviting any interested party to contact you about issues that go on in your classroom.

Second, your classroom management plan should outline the procedures of how your class will run on a daily basis. These procedures will clearly explain your stance on tardies, homework and test-taking policies, excused and unexcused absences, grading scales, etc. Whatever you decide to include should clearly spell out what is expected in your class. I would suggest that you allow at least one teacher, one parent and one student read a draft to ensure clarity. You should solicit their suggestions and incorporate any necessary changes so your procedures are very clear for all stakeholders.

Third, you should have a section that discusses how classroom management issues will be handled in your classroom. I suggest you review the questions posed earlier in this chapter. Once you have had an opportunity to review these questions, I strongly urge you to ensure your management plan provides answers to each of these items. This is especially important because this protects you as a teacher. Also, this will let the administration at your school site, specifically the principal; know that you have thought through these items.

Finally, I would suggest that you have a section where the student and their parent/guardian sign to show that they have fully read and understand this document. This will also protect you because it shows that your students and their parents have agreed to abide by the policies and procedures of your classroom. I would suggest you give this to your students on the first day of school and have the student and the parent/guardian sign and return it to you by the end of the first week. Then, you should file each of these in a secure place so you can have access to it in the future.

Consistency with Expectations

Now that your classroom management plan is completed, make sure you are consistent with the policies and procedures of the school district/school. Students, particularly African American students, do not mind you having these policies and procedures; however, they want to know that you will follow through in the classroom on a daily basis. I would suggest from the first day of class, when the classroom teacher explains these policies and procedures that they immediately begin to follow through on whatever actions were spelled out as consequences.

Teachers, we must understand that if you are not consistent with these policies and procedures, students, particularly your African American students, will let you know that you are not being fair. With a quality management plan in place, you cannot have favorites where you parcel out discipline according to who you like. Teachers, your credibility is on the line with your students. If your students, particularly your African American students have lost confidence in your ability to properly manage the class; oftentimes, you will have some students act out even more because they want you to handle management issues.

Now, as I discuss consistency with expectations, I do not want to just focus on management issues. I want to focus on procedural issues as well. In your classroom management plan, it should clearly spell out how your classroom should flow from a procedural standpoint. For example, if we focus on your homework policies and procedures: do all students in your classroom know the formatting of how homework should be done, when it should be turned in, etc.? Given this, Table 2 outlines what you should consider for your homework policies.

Table 2: Ideas to Consider for Homework Policies

Ideas to Consider for Homework Policies
1. The formatting of homework (i.e., specifics on whether it should be typed or handwritten, etc.);
2. Place in the classroom where homework should be submitted;
3. Documentation on point value of each homework assignment;
4. A reasonable expectation as to when they will receive a grade for their homework.
5. Documentation of ramifications if homework is not turned in.
6. Documentation of ramifications if homework is turned in late.

Homework is just an example of one situation that should be clearly spelled out for your students. By providing this type of specificity, you can alleviate a variety of issues before they even occur because the students know the consequences of their actions in your classroom.

First Week of School

The first day and first week of school are always filled with various emotions (e.g., excitement, anticipation, nervousness, fear, restlessness, etc.) in schools and classrooms all across the country. Nevertheless, for your classroom to be able to run effectively, you must begin implementing your classroom strategies on the first day your students walk into your classroom. Various books and journal articles in the education research field note that if you do not win the management battle on the first day of school, it will be much harder for you to gain control of the classroom later.

So, when your students walk into the classroom on the first day of school, immediately start the process of various policies and procedures in your classroom. For example, you should clearly state the seating arrangement for your classroom. If you have selected assigned seating for your classroom to run effectively, you should immediately inform students of where they should go in the classroom based on this arrangement.

If your classroom management plan allows students to select any seat, the first day of class is the proper time to let them know that you are happy to have them to select their own seating. No matter what approach you have taken to have your students seated in the classroom, the most important aspect is that students know what to do. Before the close of this chapter, I will provide examples of seating arrangements that you may want to consider for your classroom.

Starting Class

Now that you have all students seated, you are ready to begin class. I would suggest that you welcome students to your class and inform them how excited and honored you are to have them as your students. After brief introductions, you should begin a thorough review of your classroom management plan. The majority of the first class period should be spent on this document. It is also necessary to review every aspect of the management plan and ask students if they have any questions related to the rules and expectations regarding how the classroom will operate. Once you have answered all of the questions from students, you should give each of them a copy of the management plan to take home to their parent or guardian to sign.

Before students leave class on the first day, I would suggest having them fill out a data sheet with all of their pertinent information. This information should include the following: (a) name; (b) home phone number; (c) cell phone (for parents and students); (d) student e-mail address; (e) parent e-mail address; (f) emergency contact number; (g) home address etc.; (h) Facebook, Twitter and/or Instagram page (if applicable). Your data sheet may look something like this:

Table 3: Student Data Sheet

Student Data Sheet
Name: _____
Home #: _____ Cell #_____
Cell # Parent/Guardian _____
Student E-mail (if applicable)_____
Parent E-mail: _____
Emergency Contact_____
Home Address_____
City/State_____
Facebook or Twitter page_____

Teachers, I want you to understand that it is vital that you obtain this data on the first day students are in your class. With this in mind, this is probably the only day all of the students will provide you with the correct contact information for their parents/guardians. Once you receive this information from students, please make sure you file this information away for later use. Trust me, you will need it again over the course of the academic semester or school year! Now that you have this information, our next step is to make contact with every student's parents or guardian before the end of the first week of school.

<u>First Week – Calling All Parents and Guardians</u>

We have made it to the first week of school. I know this is when all educators are extremely busy and feel like they are pulled in so many different directions. However, your assignment is to make sure you call every parent/guardian of every one of your students. The importance of this is to find out the person who can handle "Discipline from a Distance" (DFD). Discipline from a Distance is a concept that I have named that will be key to your success.

Discipline from a Distance (DFD) is especially important because the family member who handles discipline, especially in the African American community, may not be able to visit the school on a daily basis and may be unable to come to school for Parent/Teacher Association or Parent/Teacher Association meetings. However, when you have a problem with a student, they usually can handle the discipline problem from a distance, usually by telephone. Here is an example of what I am referring to:

Hello, may I speak to <u>Name of person that can handle DFD</u>. How are you today? I'm sorry to bother you at work or at home but I wanted to introduce myself. My name is <u>your name here</u> and I will be your child's teacher this school year. I just wanted to take time to connect with you to let you know how excited I am to have <u>Student's Name</u> in my classroom. I'm sure we will not have any problems as <u>Student's Name</u> seems like a very bright student. I wanted to know if I could touch base with you periodically throughout the semester to let you know how <u>Student's Name</u> is doing in my classroom. I know you are very busy. I thank you for your time.

Now, should you ever have any problem from this student you can call this person again who can possibly handle Discipline from a Distance (DFD). If that student gives you trouble in the classroom and you can't solve the issue yourself, you can call their parent/guardian using the following phone script:

Hello, may I speak to <u>Name of person that can handle DFD</u>. How are you today? My name is <u>your name here</u>. I'm sorry to bother you, however, I wanted to see if I could get your assistance. If you recall, we spoke at the beginning of the school year. Well, the reason for my call is that I've been having problems with <u>student name</u> and I have been unsuccessful in solving the classroom management issue with him/her. I was wondering if you would be willing to speak with <u>student name</u> on the phone. I have him/her right here in my classroom and would like to have this issue solved as soon as possible so we can move forward and get refocused on the coursework. Can I give him/her the phone for you to speak to him/her?

At this point, you will be able to solve 90 percent of your classroom issues just by doing this. However, my main focal point of this section of the chapter is that you have to be willing to call during the first week of the school year or the academic semester. Even if you have a large number of students, it is so important that you call because students need to clearly understand what you expect of them in your classroom.

Seating Arrangements

Educators, teachers in particular, I cannot stress enough the importance of using seating arrangements in your classroom. Seating arrangements play a critical role in solving classroom management issues. For students, particularly African American students, I would suggest that you separate them from their friends so they will not be tempted to act out. Use some sort of seating chart (you can find various examples on the Internet) that is displayed in a central place when students enter your classroom on the first day of class. Once students know their assigned seats, you can make necessary adjustments during the school year. Further, these seating arrangements will show that you are proactive in your classroom management plan.

Classroom Arrangement

In many schools across the United States, the classroom arrangement still reveals the look of a classroom of the early 1900s. Teachers, you should consider before the school year or a new academic semester, the best classroom arrangement that will work for you and your teaching style. Also, you want to find a balance in the classroom set-up based on the learning styles of your students.

As you think about your classroom arrangement, remember, most African American students do well in classrooms that allow room for movement and hands-on activities throughout the classroom. Based on this, you should seek a balance in how you will set up your room considering the following criteria: (a) your teaching style; (b) students' learning style; (c) subject(s) that will be taught; (d) activities conducted in the classroom; and (e) equipment to be used in the classroom.

Based on these activities, here are a few diagrams of possible classroom arrangements. For more information - http://www.learnnc.org/lp/pages/742

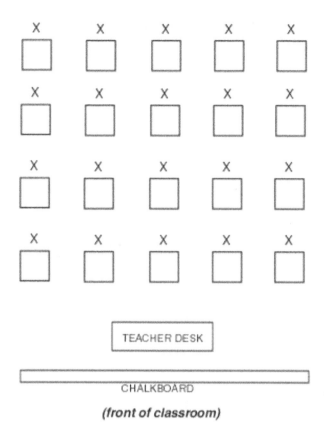

Figure 1: Traditional Classroom Setup (Katz, 2002)

A traditional classroom is often set with the desks in rows, the teacher's desk or table somewhere in front of the room and student desks moved far enough apart to prevent easy wandering of eyes during tests. This arrangement packs desks into the room efficiently and allows students to have easy access to their seats, but it certainly does not have to be the default room arrangement. The learning environment should be designed according to learning objectives and desired outcomes, not just habit or a custodian's best guess. However, this arrangement is best for controlling behavior, ensuring that there is enough space to walk, preventing cheating on traditional testing days and maintaining learning (Katz, 2002).

Centers

(front of classroom)

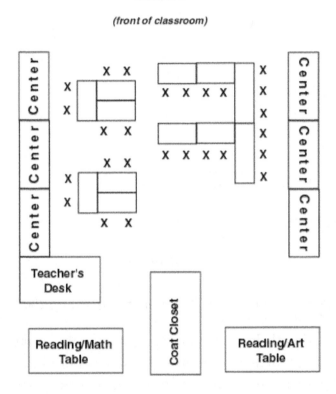

Figure 2: Classroom based on Learning Centers (Katz, 2002)

In this type of design, the teacher can take advantage of various learning centers in the classroom. This allows for movement in the classroom and has the focus more on student-centered activities versus teacher activities. If the activities in your classroom revolve around center-based activities, this may be the design for you.

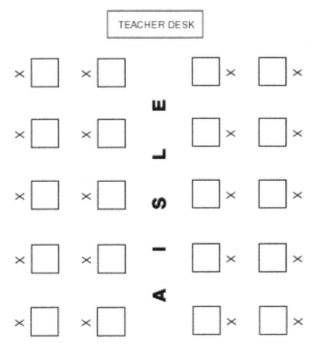

Figure 3: Classroom Design focused on Discussion/Debate (Katz, 2002)

This classroom design is geared toward teachers who have activities such as discussions/debate. This is another type of design that is focused on student-centered activities. If you look closely at this design, the teacher's area of the classroom is not the main focus. I would recommend this for teachers who are looking for students to be interactive with each other in a face-to-face format.

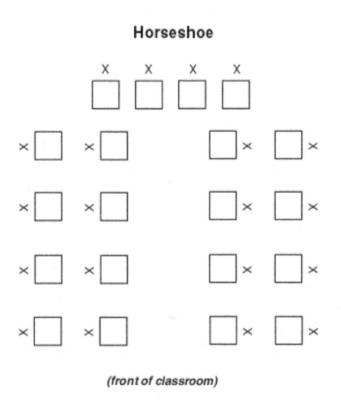

Horseshoe

(front of classroom)

Figure 4: Horseshoe Classroom Design (Katz, 2002)

Finally, this classroom design utilizes a horseshoe design. This is another option for teachers looking for student-centered activities or teacher-centered activities. In this classroom arrangement, teachers can utilize the aisle to deliver their instruction effectively. Also, students can utilize this arrangement for interactive activities as well.

In conclusion, we have covered a large amount of information in this chapter. However, I wanted to address classroom management from a variety of viewpoints because this is the main issue for most teachers in our nation's classrooms. It is my hope that this chapter is useful in assisting teachers to reach all students, particularly African American students.

Kids don't remember what you try to teach them. They remember who you are.

Jim Henson

6

Twenty (20) Strategies to Create Engaging Classrooms

We only get one chance to make a difference in the life of a child. Commit to doing it every day! Use best practices and improve!

Robert Pennington

In my many years of presenting at conferences and serving as a consultant for schools, school districts, educational organizations and many non-profit entities, the main question I receive is Dr. Lewis, can you provide us with strategies that we can use to create more engaging classrooms? As a result, I am going to write this chapter in an untraditional fashion. I am going to provide the strategy in LARGE PRINT and then write a one-paragraph summary. These strategies should be incorporated to raise the achievement levels of all of your students including your African American students.

Before I go further, I must give a special shout-out to Jawanzaa Kunjufu who has dedicated his professional career to providing strategies for educators. I suggest you check out his books, particularly the following books:

100+ Educational Strategies to Teach Children of Color (African American Images Publishing)

200+ Educational Strategies to Teach Children of Color (African American Images Publishing)

[see next page for Strategies]

Strategy #1

Culturally Relevant Teaching

Culturally Relevant Teaching has to be utilized for engaging classrooms. The key question you must ask is "can my students see their life in every lesson that I teach?" Also, you must utilize this as a way for your students to become engaged with a lesson that relates to their everyday reality. A simple formula I want you to remember that is discussed in the next chapter is:

ACADEMIC STANDARDS

+

RELEVANCE TO THE LIFE OF STUDENTS

=

CULTURALLY RELEVANT TEACHING

Strategy #2

Your Picture – Their Grade!

To get students more engaged and build better relationships with their teachers, I encourage you to bring a picture of yourself at the designated grade level(s) that you are teaching. Most students believe that you have always been the age you are now. By bringing a picture, it will be a way to break the ice and share with your students the successes and challenges you had at that grade level.

Adopted from: Kunjufu, J. (2008). 100+ Educational Strategies to Teach Children of Color. Chicago: African American Images.

Strategy #3

Student Goals by Age 30

Each teacher should have their students identify the goals they have by Age 30. By identifying these goals, you will have insight into their interests so you can incorporate into your teaching strategies. Also, you can remind them of THEIR GOALS throughout the school year to keep them focused.

Adopted from: Kunjufu, J. (2008). 100+ Educational Strategies to Teach Children of Color. Chicago: African American Images.

Strategy #4

HOMEWORK

You heard it from me! STUDENTS NEED HOMEWORK! Students have to know that you will grade their homework! Otherwise, there is no incentive. Also, the homework must be in a sweet spot that is not too easy and not too hard!

Adopted from: Kunjufu, J. (2008). 100+ Educational Strategies to Teach Children of Color. Chicago: African American Images.

Strategy #5

USE SURNAMES

For African American students, the use of surnames are very important. When you utilize surnames you are stating that I respect you enough that you actually want them engaged in the classroom. Also, in the African American community, when someone uses your surname, you know that mean business and it's time to get serious.

Adopted from: Kunjufu, J. (2008). 100+ Educational Strategies to Teach Children of Color. Chicago: African American Images.

Strategy #6

GREET STUDENTS AT THE DOOR WHEN THEY ARRIVE TO CLASS

This seems to be very simple but educators have gone away from this practice. This demonstrates to students that you really want them in the classroom. When you greet them at the door, it sets the stage for engagement.

Adopted from: Kunjufu, J. (2008). 100+ Educational Strategies to Teach Children of Color. Chicago: African American Images.

Strategy #7

WALK AND TEACH

To create engaging classrooms, you must walk and teach at the same time! Most teachers usually just stay at their desk or their designated spot to do most of their teaching. By walking and teaching, you can handle any discipline issues at the same time you are teaching.

Adopted from: Kunjufu, J. (2008). 100+ Educational Strategies to Teach Children of Color. Chicago: African American Images.

Strategy #8

PROXIMITY IN THE CLASSROOM

This is similar to Strategy #7 but when proximity is implemented, the teacher actually provides the instruction from a spot in the classroom that is 'very close' to the student that may be off-task. While teaching the lesson, the teacher can re-engage the student and get them refocused on the coursework.

Adopted from: Kunjufu, J. (2008). 100+ Educational Strategies to Teach Children of Color. Chicago: African American Images.

Strategy #9

IMPROVE YOUR REFLECTION IN THE CLASSROOM

Your students are a DERIVATE of you! If you have a negative attitude, your students will take on that personality. However, if you are EXCITED and take on a positive personality, that is what will be reflected in your classroom.

Adopted from: Kunjufu, J. (2008). 100+ Educational Strategies to Teach Children of Color. Chicago: African American Images.

Strategy #10

MORE PRAISE...LESS CRITICISM

Your students love attention. Unfortunately, too many educators spend too much time providing criticism to their students. Take the time to nurture them and watch how they will build a better relationship with you. Once they build the relationship with you, they will achieve for you!

Adopted from: Kunjufu, J. (2008). 100+ Educational Strategies to Teach Children of Color. Chicago: African American Images.

Strategy #11

EXPOSURE

To create engaging classrooms, you must EXPOSE students to experiences they have never had so it can open new learning opportunities and possibilities that they can do with their life. For example, your students may have never physically visited Niagara Falls but you EXPOSE them to it by learning about it and taking virtual tours in your class. This may spark them to want to visit one day and then they may want to start a career to develop new forms of renewable energy based on their interests and impact they want to make in the world.

Adopted from: Kunjufu, J. (2008). 100+ Educational Strategies to Teach Children of Color. Chicago: African American Images.

Strategy #12

CALL PARENTS WITH GOOD NEWS

Unfortunately, educators have built a reputation for calling parents with bad news about student behavior. However, I want you to make a concerted effort to call with good news! By doing so, you will see a student that is more confident because you made an effort to tell their parents that they did something positive.

Adopted from: Kunjufu, J. (2008). 100+ Educational Strategies to Teach Children of Color. Chicago: African American Images.

Strategy #13

TEACHERS HOLD MONTHLY PARENT MEETINGS IN THEIR ROOM WITH POTLUCK DINNER

We know food attracts parents/guardians to the school! This strategy can be used to get parents/guardians to the school so you can provide updates to them on their child(ren) progress academically. While they are in attendance, you can have ways for them to be engaged in the classroom that take 15 minutes or less. Have those tasks on a designated table for parents/guardians to pick up as they exit the classroom. Watch your parent engagement increase!

Adopted from: Kunjufu, J. (2008). 100+ Educational Strategies to Teach Children of Color. Chicago: African American Images.

Strategy #14

START A BUSINESS DRESS UP DAY

To get students more engaged, you can start a business dress-up day. This can be used in combination with Strategy #3. When students can dress-up in the attire for the career they want to pursue, it brings a new level of confidence to them. This will allow them to feel better about themselves and want to be more engaged. If they do not have the attire, work with your school partners to get the clothes donated.

Adopted from: Kunjufu, J. (2008). 100+ Educational Strategies to Teach Children of Color. Chicago: African American Images.

Strategy #15

ASK STUDENTS TO BRING A CURRENT PHOTO

By bringing a current photo, you can establish a WALL OF FAME. You can tell students that you are going to showcase them because they will be engaged and will be future leaders that will change the world!

Adopted from: Kunjufu, J. (2008). 100+ Educational Strategies to Teach Children of Color. Chicago: African American Images.

Strategy #16

SMOOTH MUSIC PLAYING IN THE BACKGROUND

I encourage all educators to have positive smooth music, like Jazz, playing in the classroom when students arrive and when they are working on assignments. This will expose them to new genres of music and keep them calm and focused as they complete their work.

Adopted from: Kunjufu, J. (2008). 100+ Educational Strategies to Teach Children of Color. Chicago: African American Images.

Strategy #17

DAILY WARM-UP ACTIVITY UPON ENTERING THE CLASSROOM

After you complete Strategy #6, I want you to have a daily warmup activity that your students complete every day that takes approximately 5 minutes. This will allow you time to check the class roster and do other logistical items before you begin the lesson for the day.

Adopted from: Kunjufu, J. (2008). 100+ Educational Strategies to Teach Children of Color. Chicago: African American Images.

Strategy #18

GIFTED AND TALENTED AREA IN THE CLASSROOM

This is a designated area in the classroom that you reserve for students that want to go HIGHER or above and beyond the expectations. You must sell this as an area where all students should strive to get to and should be a destination for each student. You have to incentivize this sacred space!

Adopted from: Kunjufu, J. (2008). 100+ Educational Strategies to Teach Children of Color. Chicago: African American Images.

Strategy #19

TEACH STUDENTS ABOUT WRITING A BUSINESS PLAN

Each student has a unique talent and can change the world. Take time to show students how they can start a business based on their talent. Tell them they have to be a solution to some issue in the world. Their business can be the business that changes the world. Start now by having them think about that business and put a plan together!

Adopted from: Kunjufu, J. (2008). 100+ Educational Strategies to Teach Children of Color. Chicago: African American Images.

Strategy #20

WEEKLY ACADEMIC CONTESTS

Students love friendly competition. Find ways to have weekly academic contests because it pushes students to become better. Don't just have the same contests every week like a Spelling Bee. Vary your approach and watch the kids excel.

Adopted from: Kunjufu, J. (2008). 100+ Educational Strategies to Teach Children of Color. Chicago: African American Images.

In closing, I want you to uses these 20 strategies daily to make a difference in the lives of the students. By incorporating these strategies, we will see all students but particularly African American students reach higher levels of academic achievement. Remember engagement produces achievement!

In learning you will teach, and in teaching you will learn.

Phil Collins

7

Culturally Relevant Teaching: Strategies for Implementation

Remember that the burden is on you to change the nature of the relationship and build trust between you and your students.

Zaretta Hammond

Educators, whether you are ready or not, your schools are going to continue to become more and more diverse culturally, racially and linguistically. As a result, your ability to meet the academic needs of all of your students will be how you and your school will ultimately be judged as successful or not. Unfortunately, with over 500 failing schools in every state (U.S. Department of Education, 2019) with D and F ratings, there must be a change in our instructional approaches that meet the needs of students of color, particularly African American students. Unfortunately, by many academic barometers, these students are struggling the most inside of the school because their academic needs are not being met in a way that is conducive for them to reach their full academic potential. As a result, I had to write this chapter for educators in the trenches basically to know how to implement Culturally Relevant Teaching (CRT) in their classroom. Let's take the journey.

Before we begin the journey on how to implement CRT, I must pay much respect to Dr. Gloria Ladson Billings and William 'Bill' Tate for this ground-breaking work with their article entitled, *"Towards a Conceptual Framework of Culturally Relevant Pedagogy: An Overview of the Conceptual and Theoretical Literature."* Dr. Ladson-Billings has written extensively about this topic and I would recommend that you study that work so you can have a firm foundation in understanding the theoretical underpinnings of this work. I highly recommend a book chapter by Dr. Ladson-Billings in one of my previous books, *White Teachers: Diverse Classrooms: Creating Inclusive Schools, Building on Students' Diversity and Providing True Educational Equity.* The name of her chapter is *Culturally Relevant Pedagogy: How Do I Do It?* This will help you understand further the body of work around this topic.

Finally, I cannot leave out the ground-breaking work of Geneva Gay and her book entitled *Culturally Responsive Teaching: Theory, Research and Practice.* After you have read each of these titles, you will have a greater appreciation for why this work is so important continues to grow into what we now call Culturally Sustaining Pedagogy.

For clarity purposes, I will use the term Culturally Relevant Teaching since that term is the most familiar in name.

Implementing Culturally Relevant Teaching

The most common question I receive as I travel across the country is: Can I implement Culturally Relevant Teaching (CRT) and still meet my academic standards in my required state curriculum? The answer is an overwhelming YES! The next statement I receive is, "I have heard of CRT but no one has shown me how to implement it." As a result, this is why I want us to make this practical as possible for you to implement in your classroom.

Practical Steps for Implementation of CRT

As we navigate this journey, I am going to provide you with the formula for success and then provide you with two examples that can serve as guide for implementation in the classroom.

ACADEMIC STANDARDS

+

RELEVANCE TO THE LIFE OF STUDENTS

=

CULTURALLY RELEVANT TEACHING

This formula is what you can use to implement CRT in any grade level with any academic standard. This is important for you to understand. In this formula, the Academic Standards are the required standards by your respective State that you are required to meet in your curriculum. So, this is what your students should learn from you as an educator. The second part of the formula is the relevancy to the life of your students. To make this even more basic, ask yourself the following question anytime you teach a lesson, *"Can your students see their life in every lesson that you teach?"* By combining the Academic Standards and Culturally Relevancy you have the foundation needed for CRT.

> ## Can your students see their life in every lesson that you teach?

Example

I am going to provide two (2) examples to illustrate how this can work in your school and in your classroom. I have thousands of examples that I can share at your school/school district/organization and assist your educators and work with them extensively on the development, implementation and assessment of lessons.

Mathematics Standard – 3rd grade (focus on Multiplication)

Fluently multiply and divide within 100...By the end of grade 3, know from memory all products of two one-digit numbers.

In the academic standard above, this is what you see as an educator. Our job is to turn this into an exciting lesson for students. Given our human tendencies, we will usually revert to what we normally do when we learned multiplication. For example, we will use the "Drill & Kill" approach where have students write our multiplication facts 1000 times until it is forced into their brains! Some of us would use manipulatives, flash cards or other educational tools to teach this concept of multiplication. All of these are fine to lay a foundation but what else will you add to this lesson to make it relevant and make it stick or be transferable for students in their everyday life. As a result, I want us to refer back to the formula I provided:

ACADEMIC STANDARDS

+

RELEVANCE TO THE LIFE OF STUDENTS

=

CULTURALLY RELEVANT TEACHING

Now, the question is how will you make multiplication "Culturally Relevant" for all of your students? This is where you are as an educator have to put in the work to sit back and think through this approach. So, here is an example for your consideration that brings together multiplication as a culturally relevant example that all of your students know. It's based on a famous restaurant that they all know – **McDonald's.**

Average Cost of Value Meals	# Sold	Answer	Student Hourly Pay	Hours Worked	Answer
$5.00	2,000/day ?/week ?/month ?/year		$8/hour	20/week ?/month ?/year	

Let's work out this multiplication problem. Remember, the goal is to check to see if the students can do the multiplication.

- Step 1: If the average price of value meals is $5.00 and they sell an average of 2,000 values meals per day. How much would they make at this one McDonald's on just value meals?

  $5.00 x 2,000 Value Meals = $_____

- Step 2: Since McDonald's is open 7 days per week, how much do they make on value meals per week?

  $[Insert Step 1 answer] x 7 days per week = $_____.

- Step 3: Assuming a 4-week month; how much does this one McDonald's make on just Value Meals?

  $[Insert Step 2 answer] x 7 days per week = $_____.

- Step 4: Since there are 12 months in a year, how much will this McDonald's make per year?
  $[Insert Step 3 answer] x 12 months per year = $_____.

- Step 5: To provide even more detail, what if I were to hire one of your students that is of high school age but I didn't even start them at minimum wage? Let's say I start them at $8 per hour but they can work only 20 hours per week because they are a high school student. How much would they make per week at McDonald's before taxes?

  $8.00 per hour x 20 hours per week = $_____.

- <u>Step 6</u>: Assuming a 4-week month, how much would they make per month at this one McDonald's?

  $[Insert Step 5 answer] x 4 weeks per month = $_____.

- <u>Step 7</u>: Given that there are 12 months in a year, how much would the make per year?

  $[Insert Step 6 answer] x 12 months per year = $_____.

In summary, educators what can we deduce from this quick Culturally Relevant lesson on multiplication utilizing mathematics? First, we must know if the students can even do the multiplication to complete the problem. Then, have the students tell you what life lessons they could have learned from this quick Culturally Relevant lesson. List 5 life lessons that students could have learned from this lesson.

- Life Lesson 1: _____

- Life Lesson 2: _____

- Life Lesson 3: _____

- Life Lesson 4: _____

- Life Lesson 5: _____

English/Language Arts Standard – 6th grade (focus on writing of poetry)

Since many critics of Culturally Relevant Teaching (CRT) note that it only works with content areas such as mathematics, let's explore how this can work with another academic subject – English/Language Arts. I know many of you have African American students that are struggling with their writing skills. Let's explore how we can take something that they really love – music and utilize it to improve their writing skills.

Here is the academic standard that will work with:

Compare and contrast the experience of reading a story, drama or poem to listening to or viewing an audio, video or live version of the text, including contrasting what they "see" and "hear" when reading the text to what they perceive when they listen or watch.

Now, if we examine this academic standard, we have to wonder how can we bring this standard to life for students? We must understand that students love their music (even though we may not always agree with or know what their music is saying)! Here is the formula again followed by the steps we can use to make it into a culturally relevant lesson.

ACADEMIC STANDARDS
+
RELEVANCE TO THE LIFE OF STUDENTS
=
CULTURALLY RELEVANT TEACHING

- Step 1: Ask your students to bring in the lyrics to their favorite song – THE CLEAN VERSION!

- Step 2: You can inform the students that they will use the lyrics to their favorite song to improve writing and even to introduce poetry.

- Step 3: Have students re-write the lyrics of their favorite song utilizing proper subject/verb agreement without losing the meaning of the song.

- Step 4: Have the students utilize only the instrumental version of the song to do a re-enactment of rapping or singing the song with the new lyrics they just created.

- Step 5: Allow students to create their own music video based on the revised lyrics they made with the writing portion of the lesson.

- Step 6. Review and summarize learning of the lesson.

To summarize, what you have done in this example is allowed the students to meet all components of this academic standard. As an educator, you were most concerned with their ability to meet the academic standards. The students were most concerned with connecting their learning to their everyday reality. Once we have a connection with their everyday reality, we can engage students in more meaningful ways. Hopefully, these two examples will serve as an opportunity for you to build exciting and engaging lessons for your students. By doing so, you will see the academic achievement of your students increase tremendously.

I want you to utilize the formula provided in this chapter with ANY academic standard in ANY content area and in ANY grade level. Please share your success stories with me. I want to hear how you have engaged your students in entirely new ways. Feel free to email me at chance.lewis@gmail.com or visit me on the web at http://www.chancewlewis.com.

We never know which lives we influence, or when, or why?

Stephen King

8

The Current Status of African American Achievement

I n this chapter, I want to clearly paint a picture of the status of African American achievement in the United States of America. In this era of *Race to the Top Legislation,* a plethora of data is available for public consumption but most of the data is heavily skewed for a variety of reasons; especially the data that is reported by states and school districts. As a result, I want to provide the most current and reliable data on the status of African American academic achievement for the United States of America. This data is reported by the United States Department of Education, National Center for Education Statistics. More specifically, it is reported by the division on the National Assessment of Educational Progress (NAEP).

This data paints a clear picture of student achievement at critical grade levels in core content courses. Also, I provide data from ten (10) urban school districts across the country so we can also see a snapshot of achievement levels of African American students in our nation's urban schools. I truly believe this chapter is very important because we now have more data available to us than any other time in U.S. history; unfortunately, many educators do not have time or simply do not wish to look at the data for the achievement of African American students and all other students in the country for that matter. Also, if you would like more data for your state or school district, please visit the website for your state department of education.

Data Reporting

For this section of the chapter, I chose to deliberately focus on the status of African American achievement in comparison to the White counterparts. While there are many ways to report this data, I chose this way because this is usually how most educational institutions measure the achievement gap. As we lay the foundation for this book, we must clearly understand where we are as far as African American achievement.

Table 1

National Assessment of Educational Progress-Math
Grade 4 (In Percent)

Race	Below Basic	At Basic	At Proficient	At Advanced
African American	34	49	16	1
White	9	39	43	9

Source: National Assessment of Educational Progress
(2019)

In a detailed look at Table 1, we can see the achievement levels of African American and White students in Grade 4. We find that African Americans are leading the categories that are considered to be negative when it comes to academic achievement in mathematics at Grade 4. More specifically, thirty-four percent (34%) of African American students are in the Below Basic category in comparison to only nine percent (9%) of White students. Also, in the category entitled "At Basic," forty-nine percent (49%) of African American students are in this category in comparison to thirty-nine percent (39%) of White students.

Now, when we focus on the upper levels of academic achievement in Table 1, it denotes the percentage of students that have reached proficiency levels or advanced levels in Grade 4. As a reminder, remember the *No Child Left Behind Legislation* stated that all students will be at this benchmark by 2014 (U.S. Department of Education, 2007).

Let's now focus on the "At Proficient" category. We find that only sixteen percent (16%) of African Americans are "At Proficient" in comparison to forty-three percent (43%) of their White counterparts at Grade 4 Math. This is a very large gap in achievement. Finally, in the "At Advanced" category, we find that only one percent (1%) of African American 4th graders have reached this level in comparison to nine percent (9%) of their White counterparts.

Grade 8 – Mathematics

As we continue to explore the achievement gap pattern for African American students in comparison to their White counterparts, it is important for us to focus on Grade 8 as well in this content area.

Table 2

National Assessment of Educational Progress-Math Grade 8 (In Percent)

Race	Below Basic	At Basic	At Proficient	At Advanced
African American	50	37	11	1
White	17	39	33	10

Source: National Assessment of Educational Progress (2019)

Focusing on Figure 2, we find that in the "Below Basic" category fifty percent (50%) of African American Grade 8 students are represented in comparison to only seventeen percent (17%) of White students. We find that this is a thirty-three (33) percentage point differential between African American students and White students in the "Below Basic" category. In the "At Basic" category, we find that African American students have a representation of thirty-seven percent (37%) of 8th grade students in comparison to thirty-nine percent (39%) of White students, which is a two (2) percentage point differential.

In the "At Proficient" category, African American students comprise only eleven percent (11%) in comparison to thirty-three (33%) of White students. It is interesting to note that African American students have a twenty-two (22) percentage point differential in this category where all students should be achieving. Finally, in the "At Advanced" category, we find that only one percent (1%) of African American students are represented in comparison to ten percent (10%) of White students. This is a nine (9) percentage point differential.

In closing, as we examine Grade 8 achievement in the area of mathematics, it is clearly imperative that we make every effort to improve the achievement gap differential especially in the "Below Basic" category.

Grade 4 – Reading

In this section of the chapter, I want to specifically focus on the content area of Reading. As we know the ability to read is of the utmost importance in this fast-changing technological society. The ability to read for African American students is directly linked to future success in academic endeavors and in their career pursuits as well. As a result, it is critical for us to understand where African American students in the nation's public schools are achieving at this current time.

Table 3

National Assessment of Educational Progress-Reading Grade 4 (In Percent)

Race	Below Basic	At Basic	At Proficient	At Advanced
African American	51	32	14	2
White	23	35	32	10

Source: National Assessment of Educational Progress (2019)

In examining the "Below Basic" category, fifty-one percent (51%) of African American students are 'left behind' in this critical content area. The achievement gap at the "Below Basic" level between African American students and their White counterparts is twenty-eight (28) percentage points. Further, if we look at the "At Proficient" category, we find that only fourteen percent (14%) of African American students have reached this critical benchmark.

We must understand the seriousness of this situation because as a result of the *No Child Left Behind* and *Race to the Top* legislation led by the United States Federal Government. Finally, when we examine the "At Advanced" category, we find that only two percent (2%) of African American students have reached the "At Advanced" category. The achievement gap between African American 8th graders in Reading and their White counterparts is eight (8) percentage points. This is too small a percentage of African American students who can read fluently.

Grade 8 – Reading

Table 4

National Assessment of Educational Progress-Reading Grade 8 (In Percent)

Race	Below Basic	At Basic	At Proficient	At Advanced
African American	42	44	14	1
White	16	43	37	4

Source: National Assessment of Educational Progress (2019)

When we focus on Grade 8-Reading achievement for African American students, we find as they matriculate through our nation's public schools that their academic achievement, in many cases, decreases year after year. The same holds true at this grade level. While there are a variety of ways to interpret this data, here are three simple ways to understand this information: (1) 86% (42% Below Basic + 44% At Basic) of African American students are not proficient in Reading at the 8th grade level; (2) only 14% of African American 8th graders have achieved proficiency at this level; and (3) only 1% of

African Americans have reached the "At Advanced" level of proficiency at this grade level.

As I write these words, my heart is filled with sorrow because of the future dilemmas they will face in their lives as a result of this academic achievement at this grade level. Educators, now is the time to make a change for the better in our profession.

Science – Grade 4

The last major content area I would like to focus on is the area of Science. When researchers write on African American student achievement, this content area is, oftentimes, overlooked. I want to highlight this content area because this subject is a foundation for African American students who may want to be the next doctors, nurses or researchers who may find the cure for a major disease. Given this, let's examine the achievement of our African American 4th graders in the area of Science.

Table 5

National Assessment of Educational Progress-Science Grade 4 (In Percent)

Race	Below Basic	At Basic	At Proficient	At Advanced
African American	54	36	10	-
White	14	40	45	1

Source: National Assessment of Educational Progress (2019)

At the 4th grade level in the area of Science, we have a major achievement gap issue. To put it plainly, 90% (54% Below Basic + 36% At Basic) have not reached proficiency status in the area of Science at Grade 4. Stated differently, only ten percent (10%) of African American students are proficient in Science. Another important trend I find in the data was the major disparity in achievement at the "Below Basic" level. African American students have a 40 percentage point differential (54% African American students – 14% White students) at this level. Educators, in the area of Science, we have to make a change for the better.

Grade 8 – Science

Table 6

National Assessment of Educational Progress-Science Grade 4 (In Percent)

Race	Below Basic	At Basic	At Proficient	At Advanced
African American	64	27	9	-
White	21	36	40	2

Source: National Assessment of Educational Progress (2019)

When I examine the data for Grade 8-Science, all I can say is UNBELIEVEABLE. Sixty-four (64%) of African American students across the United States are in the "Below Basic" category in Science (and we are the most powerful nation in the world). Additionally, ninety-one percent (91%) of African American students have not reached proficiency status at this grade level. Educators, we have to do better in preparing African American students for academic achievement in Science.

Urban School Districts

The data presented previously in this chapter was inclusive of all school districts in the United States. As I try to paint a clear picture of African American student achievement, I want to focus specifically on urban school districts across the United States.

Grade 4 – Math (Selected Urban Districts)

Table 7

National Assessment of Educational Progress-Math Grade 4 (In Percent)

City	Race	Below Basic	At Basic	At Proficient	At Advanced
Atlanta	White	2	14	56	28
	Black	42	47	11	1
Boston	White	7	31	47	16
	Black	24	54	20	1
Chicago	White	14	34	43	9
	Black	45	42	12	-
Houston	White	4	28	51	17
	Black	25	55	20	-
Los Angeles	White	14	41	38	7
	Black	47	42	10	1
New York	White	13	37	38	13
	Black	31	50	19	1

Source: National Assessment of Educational Progress (2019)

As we look at the major urban school districts across the United States, we can clearly see how African American students are faring in Grade 4-Math. Let's now turn our attention to Grade 8-Math scores.

Table 8

National Assessment of Educational Progress-Math Grade 8 (In Percent)

City	Race	Below Basic	At Basic	At Proficient	At Advanced
Atlanta	White	5	29	47	19
	Black	50	39	10	1
Boston	White	12	27	41	20
	Black	39	40	18	3
Chicago	White	16	36	33	14
	Black	52	38	9	1
Houston	White	7	27	44	22
	Black	36	47	16	1
Los Angeles	White	23	33	31	13
	Black	64	28	8	-
New York	White	20	35	33	12
	Black	50	38	12	1

Source: National Assessment of Educational Progress (2019)

As you examine these data, I want to make sure you observe several important trends. First, the disparity between White students is astounding. Second, none of these urban school districts have higher than twenty-one percent (21%) of African American students in the proficient and advanced categories. Finally, in each of these urban school districts, at a minimum thirty-six percent (36%) of

African American students are in the "Below Basic" categories.

Reading

We now turn our attention specifically to achievement in these same urban districts in the area of Reading.

Grade 4 – Reading (Selected Urban Districts)

Table 9

National Assessment of Educational Progress-Reading Grade 4 (In Percent)

City	Race	Below Basic	At Basic	At Proficient	At Advanced
Atlanta	White	5	24	45	27
	Black	56	30	12	2
Boston	White	14	29	39	18
	Black	44	39	15	2
Chicago	White	23	33	33	12
	Black	60	29	10	1
Houston	White	12	26	40	22
	Black	51	35	13	1
Los Angeles	White	25	39	28	8
	Black	61	30	8	1
New York	White	20	29	35	16
	Black	47	33	17	3

Source: National Assessment of Educational Progress (2019)

According to Table 9, we see the trend continue on how African American students are performing in comparison to their White counterparts. It is interesting to note that out of all of these urban districts in this table, the highest percentage of African American students that were proficient were in the New York City school district with only 20% of their African American students reaching this level.

Grade 8 – Reading (Selected Urban Districts)

Table 10

National Assessment of Educational Progress-Reading Grade 8 (In Percent)

City	Race	Below Basic	At Basic	At Proficient	At Advanced
Atlanta	White	4	32	61	4
	Black	40	47	12	-
Boston	White	15	30	43	12
	Black	44	42	13	1
Chicago	White	20	39	34	7
	Black	45	42	12	1
Houston	White	8	36	50	6
	Black	42	47	11	-
Los Angeles	White	17	42	35	6
	Black	49	36	14	1
New York	White	18	45	34	4
	Black	41	43	15	1

Source: National Assessment of Educational Progress (2019)

In a thorough review of Table 10, we notice another interesting trend that I must highlight. In all the urban school districts listed in Table 10, not one has enough African Americans to make greater than one percent (1%) in the "At Advanced" category. This is an educational injustice that this group of students has not been prepared to reach the highest levels of reading achievement. Educators, we must improve the reading levels of African American students so they can make their mark on our global society.

Grade 4 – Science (Selected Urban Districts)

Table 11

National Assessment of Educational Progress-Science Grade 8 (In Percent)

City	Race	Below Basic	At Basic	At Proficient	At Advanced
Atlanta	White	4	21	71	4
	Black	56	35	9	-
Boston	White	15	42	43	1
	Black	46	43	10	-
Chicago	White	22	40	37	-
	Black	71	25	5	-
Houston	White	9	28	61	2
	Black	52	39	8	-
Los Angeles	White	24	41	36	-
	Black	64	30	6	-

		Below	At	At	At
		Basic	Basic	Proficient	Advanced
New York	White	17	42	41	1
	Black	57	34	9	-

Source: National Assessment of Educational Progress (2019)

In a review of urban school districts in the content area of Science we find that the best-case scenario for African American students reaching proficiency is the ten percent (10%) of African American students in Boston. Unfortunately, the plight for African American students does not look favorable. In each of these urban school districts, over 90% of African American students are not doing well. It is my hope that highlighting these alarming statistics will move educators to do more to properly educate this population.

Grade 8 – Science (Selected Urban Districts)

Table 12

National Assessment of Educational Progress-Science Grade 8 (In Percent)

City	Race	Below Basic	At Basic	At Proficient	At Advanced
Atlanta	White	-	-	-	-
	Black	72	22	6	-
Boston	White	26	31	42	2
	Black	74	20	6	-
Chicago	White	33	39	27	1
	Black	83	14	3	-
Houston	White	14	28	54	4
	Black	62	29	9	-

Los Angeles	White	36	34	28	1
	Black	76	20	5	-
New York	White	37	34	28	1
	Black	76	20	5	-

Source: National Assessment of Educational Progress (2019)

In Grade 8-Science, we see again that African American students have not reached the "At Advanced" category in any of the urban school districts listed in Table 12. Also, it is interesting to note that in the Atlanta urban school district, 81% of African Americans are in the "Below Basic" category. It is my hope that I see the day where all African American students reach their full academic potential.

Conclusion

In this chapter, I have tried to provide the most complete description on the status of African American students in a way that is understandable for any reader of this book. **Few authors present this information in a way that is clear to all readers.** As a result, I want all of my readers to have a clear picture on the status of African American students in our nation's schools.

Now that we know the information presented in this chapter, we must take steps to improve the achievement of African American students. Currently, African American students are at the bottom of every major academic barometer. Given that I am a product of many dedicated parents and educators, I know this population has much more potential than the data presented in this chapter. We, as educators, have to ensure we are doing our part to make positive changes for this population. Let's move forward to the subsequent chapter where we focus in on what educators can do to make a difference.

You cannot teach a man anything, you can only help him find it within himself.

Galileo

9

African American Students and Homework

The student that is going to win is the one that does their homework.

Imran Khan

A s we continue on our journey to guide you to work effectively with African American students, I feel it is very important to address the topic of homework as it relates to academic achievement in all academic content areas, particularly in urban educational settings. It is my belief that homework is one of the most underutilized resources in academic classrooms that can change the plight of African American student achievement. As a result, I would like for us to explore how to use homework more effectively to raise the skill level of African American students. To do so, I would like to address the following topics in this chapter: (a) The Importance of Homework; (b) Important Types of Homework; (c) Frequency of Homework; and (d) Homework and Overall Academic Goals.

The Importance of Homework

Homework is as important to African American students as oxygen is important to us to live on earth! To put it plainly, if teachers are not providing quality homework assignments for African American students, they are cutting off the oxygen to their academic life! For purposes of this chapter and this book, *homework* in my viewpoint is defined as an assignment that is given in class by the course instructor that should be completed outside the classroom to enhance the academic skills of the African American student. Based on this definition, I would like to explore two important points: (1) the importance of homework for the African American student and (2) the importance of homework for the classroom teacher.

> **To put it plainly, if teachers are not providing quality homework assignments for African American students, they are cutting off the oxygen to their academic life!**

The Importance of Homework for the African American Student

As I travel and visit schools/school districts across the United States, I am truly amazed that when I engage in informal conversations with African American students how many of these students tell me they rarely have homework in any of their academic courses. I often ask, "Is it that the homework was not assigned in class or is it that you did not complete your homework assignment?" Most often, these African American students tell me that they do not have homework because their teachers do not want to grade these assignments. Each time I hear this from African American students, it saddens me because I think of this as the slow academic death of the African American students, especially those in urban educational settings.

Given that the goal of this book is to guide educators to work more effectively with African American students, I want you to understand that homework is vitally important for their academic success. The time spent on homework assignments teaches several important variables that are beneficial for the remainder of their lives: (1) dedication; (2) patience; (3) time management; (4) skill development; (5) problem solving; (6) analytical skills; and (7) many other additional skills.

Unfortunately, one of the few times that that many African American students have to develop these skills is in their academic classrooms. In most situations for African American students across the United States, these academic classrooms are not the best place to develop these skills because a large majority of academic class time is dedicated to classroom management issues with the remaining class time dedicated to academic content on a surface level. In these situations, in-depth exploration into the subject matter does not happen on a frequent basis. As a result, homework is so important because it allows the African American student to practice their skills outside of the classroom so when they return to the classroom they can make steady progress towards positive academic goals.

Another reason that homework is vitally important for African American students is based on the fact that it can shape these students into better people in the future. I know you as the readers are saying; now how does this make them a better person? If you examine some of the variables I mentioned earlier (i.e., dedication, patience, time management, skill development, problem solving, analytical skills, etc.), homework can be critical in developing all of these skills. Homework, whether individual or group-based, can teach the skills of dedication, patience, time management, skill development, problem solving, analytical skills, etc. in a variety of ways.

> Homework, whether individual or group-based, can teach the skills of dedication, patience, time management, skill development, problem solving, analytical skills, etc. in a variety of ways.

First, dedication is a key skill that is shaped by homework. One fact that we are aware of as educators is that if homework is a major part of our academic outcome strategy, students will need to be dedicated to be successful in the classroom. Dedication is built by constantly facing intellectual exercises outside the classroom. Dedication is also developed by time-on-task that homework assignments provide. Webster (2016) defines dedication "as a self-sacrificing devotion." Educators, based on this definition, we have to move our African American students to spend more time completing homework.

Second, completing homework assignments teaches *patience*. According to Webster (2019), patience is defined as "steadfast despite opposition or difficulty." Similar to dedication, *patience* is learned via homework because African American students may not get the all the answers correct the first time but they can continue to develop the patience to persevere. As a result, this development of patience can assist them to figure out what they are doing wrong so they can hopefully correct it in the future.

Additionally, as African American students learn the virtue of patience, they will also learn more about themselves. I personally think that this is very rewarding. So, teachers do not stop providing the homework for African American students, or other students, as it [homework] has the potential to teach them the invaluable lesson of patience. Just think teachers, how often we must use patience.

Third, another important lesson that can be learned is time management. I think every person, including African American students, should learn this because it takes some people all of their lives to attempt to master this key variable. While your students may not be perfect in mastering this valuable skill, homework allows them to begin to develop this skill by preparing to meet deadlines, adjusting their schedules, and many other intangibles so they can have their assignments submitted in a timely fashion.

Fourth, skill development is another ability that is perfected during the homework process. Educators in many urban educational settings, African American students do not have adequate time in class to develop their academic skills to the fullest potential. As a result, it is important that teachers provide quality homework assignments that enhance these skills outside of the classroom. Further, given that so many academic subjects build on previous skills obtained, African American students must be able to work daily on those skills that are needed for the various standardized tests that they are faced with in the academic environment. This is why I highly recommend that homework is given on a frequent basis because African American students, as well as all students in the academic setting, need the necessary skill development if they are going to be competitive in the fast-changing world of the 21st century.

Fifth, another benefit of homework is the development of the skill of problem solving. Educators, we learn that if African American students are going to reach their full potential in their academic endeavors, they must become effective problem solvers. The beauty of the field of education is that homework can teach this skill. Having students develop these skills through homework assignments will also have greater benefits later in their lives as well. This is especially true when many African American students, as well as other students, leave school and cannot handle the 'real world' where they will have to solve problems. We all know that problems are all around us; however, our ability to solve these problems is firmly rooted in our ability to tap into our problem-solving skills. We must remember this skill is developed through homework.

Sixth, in close alignment with the development of the skill of problem solving, African American students must also enhance their analytical skills. Analytical skills are very important because there will be times in the academic environment and in life in general where African American students will have to use their analytical skills at the 'drop of a dime.' This usually occurs when they have to figure out numbers in their head. By this, I mean sometimes students have to figure out the cost/benefit of something in their lives. Some examples are:

1) Should I take this job?
2) Can I afford to purchase these clothes?
3) Is x greater than y?

While these are only a few examples, we see quite clearly that analytical skills are truly important for the African American student, especially if they are going to survive and prosper in the 21st century.

To conclude this section, time and space would not allow me to explain every potential benefit of homework for the African American student; however, I want to make it clear to educators that homework is a critical foundation of success if African American students are going to improve their academic standing and become 'academic warriors' (Moore, 2003).

The Importance of Homework for the Teacher

Teachers, in consulting with various schools and school districts across the United States, particularly those in urban areas, I find a sentiment from African American students that continues to bother me. Many students tell me that they are not motivated to complete their homework because, in most cases, their teachers, who are ultimately responsible for their education, will not grade all of their homework. As a result, these students feel that it is a waste of time to complete these assignments. Given this sentiment, at this point of the chapter, I want to express why I feel homework is important to teachers as well.

Homework provides you with a current status report

Teachers, we must understand that daily homework allows us to assess our students' ability. This is very important because many teachers, and other educators as well, have no idea of the academic standing of their students throughout the full grading period, particularly their African American students. In most cases, teachers deliver content over several days or weeks; however, only a few know if their students are gaining the skills necessary to complete the academic requirements of the classroom.

However, if we are going to get a clear status report, we [educators] must have adequate data to make important decisions about the African American students in our classrooms. In addition, if we are going to have this data, we must grade their homework. Without grading their homework, we will not have the necessary data to make these important decisions about their academic futures. As a case in point, let's examine two scenarios showing why obtaining data (grading their homework) is important for the teacher.

In looking at these scenarios, what do we learn from the data about each of these African American students based on this homework data? Here are some questions to consider:

1. What is the overall lesson learned just from assessing the assignments of these 5 students?

2. Should the teacher re-teach the major concepts of this lesson?

3. How does the teacher build on this for the next lesson?

Educators, however, you choose to answer these questions reveals the lens you bring to the classroom. Nevertheless, the data tells a story. You have to be willing to understand the story the data is telling you. I do not have the adequate amount of space in this book to cover this further; but, I want you to see how collecting data from homework can provide a picture of the African American students' status as well as the other students that are in your classroom.

Homework allows you to understand what to teach or re-teach

Teachers as we enter this section, I want us to explore some other benefits of assigning homework to your African American students. One of the most obvious factors that data from homework can provide is what concept we need to teach and re-teach in the classroom. Unfortunately, in many schools, educators are in such a rush to 'cover' the curriculum that they rarely provide any 'depth' and 'breadth' to the academic content. In this rush to cover the curriculum, African American students are being severely short-changed in their educational attainment. As a result, my purpose for this section of the chapter is to assist teachers in understanding that homework allows you to understand what you can teach or re-teach!

Let's look at this example: Imagine Teacher A has just taught a science lesson focused on photosynthesis to a group of middle school students. In this class, 60% of the students are African American, 15% are Hispanic and 25% are White. Teacher A gives a homework assignment where 45% of the students correctly answer 5 out of 10 questions (50%). What should the teacher do? They have basically two choices. One choice is that they can decide to move forward with the next assignment on the curriculum knowing that the next assignment builds on the current assignment. If they choose this option, the teacher knows that the likelihood of the students' success has been greatly diminished because they were not successful on the current assignment.

The second option that is available to the teacher is to decide to re-teach the lesson in a way that can assist the students in the class to master the skills of the current assignment. Unfortunately, too many teachers take the first option when it comes to African American students and other students in urban educational settings. The first option can have a detrimental effect on all the students in this class for the rest of their lives.

In closing this section, educators, we must understand that these 'silent decisions' are tearing away at the fabric of academic achievement for African American students as well as students of other ethnic backgrounds as well.

Two Types of Homework

In this section, I want to provide the reader with two (2) types of homework that I feel are important for African American students as well as all other students. They are as follows: (1) Skill Development Homework and (2) Research-Based Homework. I will now explain each of these to assist educators in understanding why these are important for African American students.

Skill Development

Educators, content-specific homework is vitally important for the academic development of African American students. For this book, content-specific homework is general homework in an academic area that develops the African American students' potential for success in their academic courses. As an example, in the content area of mathematics, skill-development is mastering review problems on skills that were taught over the previous class session by the instructor. In the content area of English, it can be homework that is focused on the development of writing skills. Basically, in each content area, African American students should have homework that is required frequently.

Educators, as we assign this homework, we must make sure that it meets the goals/objectives of our class. Also, homework should not be given that will waste the student's time without enhancing their skills. We must remember every homework assignment must lead to a larger goal of academic achievement. If this is the goal, each time we provide a homework assignment (on a frequent basis), we must make sure we assess the homework well. This is very important. However, we must remember that to increase the academic **achievement of African American students, we must provide homework that will aid in their skill development.**

Research-Based Homework

Educators, I firmly believe that we often neglect to provide our students with the second type of homework that I feel is especially important in their academic development. This is research-based homework (i.e., project-based learning). I feel this type of homework is most important in developing the analytical skills of the African American student. For purposes of this book, research-based homework is where the student has to view multiple sources to obtain the information necessary in order to complete the assignment for this class. Examples of this are research papers, science projects or any other homework activity where the student has to put in a significant amount of time gathering data, analyzing data, utilizing analytical skills to make critical decisions to produce a high-quality finished product to submit to their teachers.

It is my personal opinion that this type of homework has the most long-term benefits for the student because of the time and effort that students have to put in on these assignments. I believe because the homework assignment is hands-on, students remember these skills for a longer period of time and can apply these to other situations in the future. However, we must remember that to get students to this level of homework, they must be familiar with the first type of homework, which is the skill-based homework (see description).

Conclusion

Educators, as we close out this chapter, I want to reiterate how important homework is for the academic development for all students, in particular, African American students. In this chapter, we have explored the importance of homework for the African American student and the added benefits for the teacher. Also, we have discussed the two general categories of homework that can be provided for students as well. It is my sincere hope that the educators who need this book will assign more meaningful homework to all students, particularly African American students who need it the most. This is critical if these students are going to develop skills that will allow them to be competitive in the 21st century. If the students are our future, what have we prepared them to be?

I never teach my pupils, I only attempt to provide the conditions in which they can learn.

Albert Einstein

10

African American Students and Standardized Testing: Preparation and Performance

D*r. Lewis, can you provide my school/school district with some teaching strategies that will assist our African American students in passing the state standardized tests? By the way, we need these strategies to work in two months or less because our state standardized testing is upon us and we want to look good with this newly required common core curriculum!*

As I travel around the United States providing consulting services to many schools and school districts, I hear these same questions from many educators. In many cases, the majority of these schools and school districts want someone to come in and provide 'a quick fix' to a situation that needs a sustained effort to address. Unfortunately, many schools and school districts do not want to address some systemic issues that are taking place every day that prevent all students, particularly African American students, from reaching their full potential in their academic courses and/or state-required standardized testing.

As we move forward in this chapter, I feel it is necessary that I let the reader know my position on state-required standardized testing under the *Race to the Top Legislation*. I am a lukewarm supporter of standardized testing because for the first time in recent decades, we (the educational community, the general public and other interested stakeholders) have data on how all students are progressing in our nation's schools (including subgroups that attend these schools). However, I am not in favor of all students being required to meet the same academic standards without being provided equitable educational facilities, educational resources, quality teachers and equitable test-taking strategies to perform at a high level on these standardized tests. Until we solve these types of issues in K-12 education, we will continue to see the disparity in academic achievement, especially for African American students.

Now as we focus in on African American students and their performance on standardized tests, I would like to address the following issues in this chapter: (1) the educator's mindset about African American students' ability to perform on standardized tests; and (2) preparation needed to have African American students perform on these state-required standardized tests.

The Educator's Mindset about African American Student's Ability on Standardized Tests

Educators (teachers, administrators, counselors, social workers, etc.), I want you to know that your mindset has a direct impact on African American student's ability to perform on state-required standardized tests. Earlier in this book, I presented a quote from Jawanzaa Kunjufu (2001) which stated:

I don't become what I think I can;

I don't become what you think I can;

*I become what I think **you think** I can*

As a result, African American students and all other students know what you (the educator) think about their abilities before they even enter the testing environment. This is why it is critical that any educator who reads this book raises their expectation level of African American students in the academic environment. It is my personal opinion that the worst form of racism is the 'racism of low expectations.' Given this, it is now time for us to raise our expectation for this group of students. As we continue to prepare African American students for the state-required standardized tests, if they turn in work that is not of the quality that we expect, we should return it to these students and have it

163

redone until it meets the standards we require. We must understand that their lives depend on it.

Now as we focus on the educator's mindset as we enter the area of standardized testing, we must understand that all students, particularly African American students will be as confident as they feel their educators (administrators, teachers, counselors, etc.) are confident in them. Stated differently, they genuinely believe that their educators expect them to pass the test, that is the level at which they will perform.

For educators to clearly understand this, several conditions need to have been met to build the African American students' confidence approaching the time for state-required standardized testing: (1) Were these African American students adequately taught the skills to be successful by a competent, confident and caring group of teachers?; (2) Did the educators (administrators, teachers, counselors, etc.), at the outset, have the expectation that these African American students were going to pass this state-required standardized test?; (3) Did the teacher clearly express to all students in the class, particularly African American students, that they had confidence in their academic ability on this state-required standardized test?; (4) Did the teacher provide valuable test-taking skills that are critical in the testing environments?; and (5) Were the students encouraged to get an adequate amount of rest and a good meal before the state-required standardized tests? Even when all of these conditions are met, many African American students will have in their mind the notion of stereotype threat (see Steele & Aronson, 1997). I would encourage every educator to read this because we must have the students, especially African American students confident enough to believe they can achieve.

Also, when I think about the mindset that educators must to have, I feel it is also imperative that the schools and school districts are committed to excellence for African American students as well. By this I mean that the mindset for the school and/or school district should also be aligned to have the best academic environment for African American students. I often see so many educators in school districts that are not in education for the right reasons. In many cases, they are not doing all that they can to assist the African American student to be successful on standardized tests. Unfortunately, many of these intentional acts often go unnoticed by the school administration that is paid to oversee the educational enterprise.

In one example I can think of immediately, I know of a school and a school district that were secretly encouraging African American students to miss school on the required testing dates so their testing results could be much better because these educators felt that the "African American score would decrease the school score." When I think on this example, I see a clear picture of the mindset that is negative for African American students.

First, educators in this school district already believed that African American students were not going to pass the state-required standardized tests. Second, for the school district to look good in the short-term, they would rather compromise the long-term success of African American students. Third, the school district also has a mindset that the majority of African American students are not good test-takers and this is even more damaging to their student population because now these students will carry this stereotype for their rest of their lives whenever they face a testing environment or any other high-stakes testing situation.

In concluding this section on mindset, I want us to know that the mindsets of educators (administrators, teachers, counselors, etc.) are arguably the most powerful indicator of how well African American students will achieve in the testing environment. While I do not see an end to the state-required standardized testing environment anytime in the near future. I am greatly disturbed by the academic trajectory of African American students if the educators who are paid to make their lives better are ultimately damaging them for the future. I must note that I am not referring to all educators, only those that do not have the best interest of students at heart.

Preparing African American Students for Standardized Tests

Educators, particularly classroom teachers, we must understand that if African American students are going to perform well on standardized tests in their core content areas, they will have to be prepared well in advance. What I am promoting here is not a crash course; I am advocating preparation for standardized testing that is part of the daily classroom routine. This should occur on a daily basis inside of the classroom. Let's explore some critical elements that must be in place to facilitate success for African American students on standardized tests: (a) content knowledge; (b) application of content knowledge; and (c) test-taking skills.

Content Knowledge

I believe that at the core of the movement to have more African American males successful on the state and national standardized tests, educators, specifically classroom teachers, must increase their content knowledge in core academic subjects. I am not referring to just a surface level knowledge of content, I mean an in-depth knowledge base that is appropriate at their respective grade levels. In order for African American students to receive this level of knowledge, teachers have to be willing to set up a classroom environment that promotes learning in a way that is culturally relevant (Ladson-Billings, 2006) for African American students. Also, the teachers need strong classroom management skills so the majority of the classroom time is focused on instruction rather than discipline. This is especially important to begin to prepare all students particularly, African American students, with the type of content knowledge needed to be successful on state-required standardized tests.

Additionally, teachers must push African American students past just rote learning practices; they must be pushed on a daily basis to use higher-order thinking skills (analysis and synthesis, see Bloom's Taxonomy on Learning). Unfortunately, I truly believe this is the main reason why African American students are not doing well because they are not taught to think and be independent learners. They are basically taught to totally depend on the teacher to generate new knowledge instead of being pushed to take knowledge further and use higher-order thinking skills. Educators, we must realize that this is a critical key to success for African American students.

Application of Content Knowledge

Educators, teachers in particular, we must also understand that only having content knowledge isn't the magic formulate for success for African American students. African American students must be taught how to apply content knowledge to any given situation they may face on standardized tests. Rarely are students asked to just regurgitate content knowledge, it is more often the application of content knowledge that usually hinders even the most savvy African American students on standardized tests.

Application of content knowledge can look differently based on the context of the classroom. However, to state it as plainly as I can, all students, particularly African American students should be able to see different situations that call for them to reflect and recall the critical content knowledge of their core academic courses and appropriately use this knowledge to handle unexpected situations on standardized tests.

We must remember that the content knowledge provides the foundation and application of that content knowledge provides the ability of the African American student to increase the likelihood that they will pass the standardized tests. We must remember that application of knowledge is a major indicator if African American students will be successful on standardized tests.

Test-Taking Skills

In order for African American students to increase their success on standardized tests, we (educators) must teach these students critical test-taking skills and strategies that will be essential to their success on these types of tests. I truly believe that there is a test-taking gap between other ethnic groups and African American students, especially those students in suburban schools compared to African American students in urban schools. We know that parents of high SES (socio-economic status) students spend large amounts of money on test-taking workshops to give their students advantages that only money can buy. However, many African American students, particularly those in urban educational settings do not have the funds to attend these types of workshops. As a result, they are dependent upon their teachers to provide them with those essential skills. Unfortunately, many educators (administrators, teachers, counselors, etc.) do not equip them with the vital skills for their success.

These vital skills that I am referring to with test-taking strategies are how to answer all types of questions these students may see on state-required standardized tests (i.e., multiple choice, matching, short answer, etc.). As a single example, let's focus on a multiple-choice question that may appear on a state-required standardized test. African American students must know how the strategies for answer these types of questions work. Let's use the following example:

> *New York is a* _____.
> a. *City*
> b. *State*
> c. *Country*
> d. *All of the above*
> e. *None of the above*
> f. *Both a and b*

In this example, many African American students would look for one correct answer; however, in this situation there is more than one correct answer. African American students must be taught this simple test-taking skill that can have a great impact on their test scores on the state-required standardized tests. Also, they have to know how to handle what I call the loaded answers of 'all of the above' and/or 'none of the above.' If students are just trying to understand the concepts on the day of the state-required standardized test, I can just about guarantee that they will not do well on the standardized test.

Conclusion

In sum, we have explored quite a few issues in this chapter that have the potential to impact African American students negatively on standardized tests. I firmly believe now is the right time to make systematic change in our educational system for the benefit of African American students. We must realize that now and in the foreseeable future, state-required standardized tests will continue to be in the K-12 educational arena. I am challenging the entire field of education to put our best efforts forward in preparing African American students for academic success. I am not just referring to good intentions but I am referring to improving systematic change that will benefit African American students for many years to come. This is vitally important if this student population will even see the promises of what education has to offer.

11

Engaging African American Parents with Mobile App Technology

Information moves fast in today's society. In many ways, it's an exciting time because more people are connected to the Internet than any other time in history. Regardless of income level, more people have access to the Internet through smartphones to access the tremendous amount of information that is in the information highway. The same is true for African American students and parents in our schools. More than ever, African American students and their parents have access to cell phones. Regardless of income levels, this is true today! Unfortunately, schools have been very slow in utilizing technology to reach all students and parents, particularly those that are African American. As a result, the goal of this chapter is to introduce one of the most powerful tools to engage African American students and parents – the incorporation of a mobile app at the school and classroom level.

I must say that I bring this chapter to this book because many schools and teachers have done a poor job in communicating with parents in effective and useful ways. Additionally, innovative methods to reach today's youth has been lacking as well. This is why I bring this idea of utilizing a school and/or a classroom mobile app for consideration to effectively reach African American students and their parents/guardians (including other demographics in your school as well). I am a firm believer that if we reach them utilizing 21st century methods of engagement, they will reach new levels of excitement with academic coursework, which ultimately leads to higher academic performance. As a result, I provide examples of how schools can utilize mobile apps to reach African American students and their parents in innovative ways.

WHAT IS A MOBILE APP?

Mobile apps or mobile applications most commonly referred to as an app, is a type of application software designed to run on a mobile device, such as a smartphone or tablet computer (e.g., iPads). Mobile apps frequently serve to provide users with similar services to those accessed on personal computers. Based on this definition, schools can put the power of mobile apps to use by incorporating mobile app technology into their everyday operations by placing the information at the fingertips of students and parents since the majority of them use their cell phones constantly. Let's walk through the process of getting a mobile app implemented in the school.

Step #1: Implement or Update Your Website

The first step that your school needs to consider is to either have a website built or updated for your school. In today's 21st century, your website is very important. The more up-to-date the website the better. Your mobile app developer will need the information on your website to build a provide a large portion of the content for your mobile app. Provide your mobile app developer with the website of the school to begin the process.

Step 2: Mobile App Development Begins

Once you provide an updated website to your mobile app provider, they will start the process to developing a high-quality mobile app for your school. In this phase, the mobile app developer will enlist the services of their graphic designers to build an aesthetically pleasing mobile app based on the graphical themes and content of your website. After the completion of the building of the app, they usually provide the opportunity for selected school personnel to preview the mobile app before it is loaded to the App Store (for all Apple products, i.e., iPhones, iPads, etc.) or the Google Play store for all Android devices. After the preview period, in most cases, your mobile app provider should have your mobile app ready for worldwide downloading in approximately four (4) weeks.

Step 3: Training Period for School Designee

After the mobile app is available for worldwide downloading, most mobile app providers provide a training period for selected personnel at your school that will be responsible for controlling the content on the mobile app. The majority of mobile app providers will have some form of training available for these selected personnel. This training should get these designated individuals familiar with the mobile app technology so they can customize as needed and then prepare a marketing plan to roll out to the school to engage students and parents.

Step 4: Marketing the New Mobile App at Your School or Classroom

Educators, it is highly important that we effectively market our mobile app to our stakeholders (i.e., parents, students and other stakeholders). Our mobile apps are only as powerful as our ability to get our stakeholders to download them to their smartphones and other electronic devices. This is important because once they download the mobile app, we will have access to reach them 24 hours a day and 7 days a week to disseminate and receive information.

Step 5: Welcoming Your School or Class Community to Your New Mobile App

Congratulations! Your school or class community has now downloaded your new mobile app. You have provided the power of technology right in the palm of their hands. Now that we have the power in their hands, it will be important that you communicate with them early and often so they can have the impression that this is one of the most important tools that is available to them. Below, we will briefly review a few of the key features of the majority of ways mobile apps that can be used for your school or classroom:

Pop-Up Messages & Instant Alerts

Mobile app technology allows you the ability to send pop-up messages and instant alerts (commonly known as push notifications) to parents, guardians, and other stakeholders of upcoming events or event changes/cancellations. This will allow parents to know instantly about events and school closures/emergencies or any other events that are important for them to know instantly.

Absentee Notes on the Go – Hassle Free!

Your mobile app can provide parents with the ability to submit sick notes and absentee information from all smart devices. Additionally, it will allow office staff to have more time to dedicate to important tasks.

Publish School or Class Newsletters

Newsletters can now be sent and read by parents on the go! It doesn't matter if they are in the carpool line or at their child's after-school activities. This convenience increases parent involvement in the events of the school/classroom and reduces paperwork that parents need to keep up with.

Locate School Activities and Events with Google Maps

Mobile app technology helps parents know where activities or events are located right on their smartphones. As a beautiful feature, Google Maps can pinpoint all venues used by schools avoiding the sight of lost, stressed parents on their way to a school event.

Integration of Social Media & On-Line Payments

Mobile apps will allow your school or classroom to integrate any on-line payment system (i.e., PayPal) and social media (i.e., FaceBook, Twitter, etc.) directly into the mobile app. Your classroom parents and other stakeholders can have access to what they need to pay for items and have access to social media platforms. There is no need to mail checks when everything can be handled from the phone.

Conclusion

So, what does this mean for educating African American students and getting involvement from their parents? Too often we hear from schools about parental involvement from families of African American students. This is because we are communicating from the school in archaic ways. Given that we are in the 21st century, it is now time for us to communicate that way. Educators, we must remember that most parents/guardians in today's society have a smartphone. It is up to our schools to make sure that we are able to get information to parents and stakeholders to ensure the success of their children.

If your school is interested in incorporating mobile app technology, please contact me for mobile app solutions for your schools at chance.lewis@gmail.com.

The aim of the college, for the individual student, is to eliminate the need in his life for the college; the task is to help him become a self-educating man.

George Lorimer

12

The Expectation of College

Here's an interesting thought, "what if we prepared all students as if they were attending college or some other postsecondary institution?" I know that some educators reading this book may see this as idealistic thinking on my part; however, I truly feel that many educators' expectations of African American students are too low. Unfortunately, in many K-12 settings, educators make the decision that early in a student's life of what they will do after high school. Also, I do not think it is for educators to decide who will and who will not go to college.

We (educators) should prepare all students, including African American students as if they are going to attend college or some other postsecondary option. Then, we should let the African American decide whether they will pursue this option in their lives! As a result, this chapter is written to educators with a purpose to change the mindset about the future of African American students. More specifically, it is the goal of this chapter to establish a 'new normal' expectation of college for the African American students and all other students in K-12 educational settings, particularly those students in urban schools.

Postsecondary Education as the 'New Normal' Expectation

Educators, as we are in a new day and time, where we are responsible for preparing students to be competitive in a global economy of the 21st century, we have a unique opportunity to make a difference in the lives of so many of our students. Also, we have the unique challenge of preparing all students, particularly African American students, for jobs that are not even created yet. Given this unique and exciting time in history, it is understood that a high school education will no longer suffice as the end of educational training needed to be competitive in this global economy. As a result, I want us (educators) to think of a postsecondary education (i.e., college, university community college, junior college, trade school, etc.) as the 'new normal' expectation for all students, particularly African American students.

As African American students enter the classrooms of our nation's schools, we must develop every lesson plan, every academic activity, every assessment and every extracurricular activity with the expectation that these students will pursue postsecondary options. It is absolutely critical that the school district, building administrators, counselors and teachers relay the same message that postsecondary education is the 'new normal' for all students.

Also, all evaluation of these employees should be made on the basis of how well they are preparing these students for this expectation. If we do not take this on as the 'new normal' expectation, we will continue to supply our society with African American students and students from other ethnic groups that are unprepared or underprepared to take on the demands of the 21st century. As we know, when African American students are unprepared or underprepared leaving our K-12 public schools, we have set them up for a life of 'societal failure' and total dependence on governmental services. It will be especially hard for them to break out of this cycle to be independent productive members of society. As a result, we can provide 'preventive maintenance' and prepare these students early to pursue additional postsecondary options after high school so they can change the future trajectory of their lives and the lives of their families.

Another reason why it is vitally important that postsecondary education is the 'new normal' expectation is because of a theory of what I call the *Lewis Theory of Box Mobility.* In this *Lewis Theory of Box Mobility,* we find that in the United States, cities are usually classified as one of three city types: (1) urban; (2) suburban; or (3) rural. According to the U.S. Census, urban areas are defined as 1,000 or more people per square mile (note more boxes in the urban box). Suburban city types are classified as 500 – 999 people per square mile (note less boxes than urban settings more than rural settings). Rural settings are definite as 0 – 499 people per square mile (note the least amount of boxes in this area).

Many African American students enter our K-12 public schools from the urban box. For many of these students, their entire lives and the lives of generations of their families before them have been lived and experienced inside of this same urban setting. Let me be crystal clear, nothing is wrong with any area; however, by having high expectations for African American students in the urban school setting allows these students to be exposed to life in maybe a different way. This is especially important because many African American students have not been exposed to other urban areas, suburban areas or rural areas. However, through a quality education that puts postsecondary education at the forefront of the expectations, these students will have what I call *Box Mobility*. This simply means that when these students complete their K-12 and postsecondary education, they have the ability to move/live/start businesses, etc. in whatever box they so choose. In layman's terms, they now have more options.

As an example, they can choose to stay in the urban box and restore their communities. Another option is that they can move with their families to enjoy all of the wonderful living opportunities in the suburbs. Also, they can choose to enjoy the benefits of country-style living in rural areas. While I have only listed a few ways that African American students can benefit from the *Lewis Theory of Box Mobility,* there is a plethora of other ways this theory can benefit them in their lives. However, we must understand that for the *Lewis Theory of Box Mobility* to be effective, African American students must receive a quality education that is based on academic excellence with the expectation of postsecondary education. This has direct implications for their lives and indirect implications for society-at-large.

When there is an expectation of college from the outset of their schooling experience, African American students will be able to greatly benefit from the *Lewis Theory of Box Mobility.* We must understand that when we expect great things from African American students this is when they will produce great things. It is my opinion that our expectations of African American students have been too low and we are now reaping what we expected.

Money is usually attracted, not pursued.

Jim Rohn

13

A Valuable Education: Financial Literacy for African American Students (Bonus Chapter)

Educators, as we reach the final chapter of this book, I feel it is very important to address a topic that is critically important to the long-term success of African American students. This is a firm understanding of financial literacy. I consider it absolutely appalling that all students, particularly African American students, can matriculate their entire K-12 schooling experience without learning anything about financial literacy. We must understand that after high school, African American students not only need content knowledge to pass standardized tests but also practical knowledge is needed for these students to have a firm understanding of financial literacy as well.

This knowledge that students should have obtained upon leaving school can totally shape the type of life they live after high school. Based on the fact that students are totally dependent on this type of knowledge, if schools do not begin to provide students with this valuable information, I greatly consider it a disservice to society and a greater disservice to the students that schools serve, in particular African American students.

African Americans and Financial Literacy

In many African American communities, students leave our nation's K-12 schools without a firm foundation of financial literacy. In many, but not all, African American communities, this is an unfortunate situation because many previous generations of these same students have not been taught financial literacy in a way to prove to be a positive situation to increase the financial knowledge and future wealth of their families and communities. To exacerbate this problem even further, African Americans spend the most of their disposable income on items that considered 'depreciable' items. As a result, many in the African American community are plagued by high credit card debt, low savings rates and low ratios of homeownership.

At the time of this writing, we are currently in a recession in the United States and many other ethnic communities are facing some of the same issues; however, the African American community is hit even harder by this recession (see Lewis & Erskine, 2008). As a result, it is critical that schools prepare African American students to be productive and financially literate for the global society in which they live.

Another important reason that financial literacy is essential is that when many of these African American students move on to postsecondary schools or enter the workforce immediately after high school, they are going to be face with a barrage of financial decisions that they will need to make for their financial futures. First, African American students are clearly going to have to understand how credit cards work. When African American students turn 18 years of age, they are going to have to face numerous offers from credit card companies (these offers are now coming to students in high school). These credit card companies clearly understand who they want to target and the strategies to get young naïve young adults to sign up for credit cards without a full understanding the ramifications of *Buy Now and Pay Later.*

As a result, this young, naïve adult, who has left school with a firm foundation in financial literacy is now receiving their first credit card with a $500 - $5,000 credit limit with no understanding how compounding interest works, billing cycles, Annual Percentage Rates (APR) and the impact of late payments on credit scores. By the time many of these students reach 21 years of age they already have a lifetime of debt. This is especially important to understand because many of these same African American students may not have people in their family that can 'step in' and bail them out of this debt they have accumulated. When this occurs, many people in American society tell them to work harder for higher pay without addressing the root cause of the issues, which basically is the need to have a firm foundation in financial literacy.

Second, African American students need a firm foundation of financial literacy to understand the differences between assets and liabilities. Unfortunately, K-12 students and many adults do not understand these basic principles. As a result, this is why we are seeing so much uncontrollable debt in the United States society. To make this plain and simple, African American students must firmly grasp the following principles:

Figure 1

Assets	Liabilities
Add money into your pocket and increase your Net Worth	Removes money from your pocket and decreases your Net Worth

Key Formula

Assets – Liabilities = Net Worth
(For more information, I recommend the book *Rich Dad, Poor Dad)*

In Figure 1 above, we see this in its simplest form that Assets provide the individual with money. Conversely, Liabilities decrease the amount of money that a person keeps in their possession. As a result, the formula of Assets – Liabilities = Net

Worth is critical for all students, particularly African American students to understand. Many people (i.e., bankers, family members, etc.) in society try to twist the basic definition of these two terms; however, at the most basic level, if African American students can understand these basic definitions, they can go a long way in providing a true education for students.

I must say that I was really fortunate to have an accounting class in high school by a truly phenomenal teacher named Mrs. Brenda C. Davis. After this course, I left with a clear understanding of assets, liabilities and net worth. Also, I left with a firm understanding of how to balance a checkbook. All of these are skills I use on a daily basis, which has far greater benefit to me than some of the other content I learned in my other courses.

Last, I feel that students, particularly African American students, should not leave high school without a firm foundation and understanding of how to balance and reconcile a bank account. I truly believe lacking this skill, above all others, is why so many Americans, particularly African Americans fall into deep debt. In simple terms, we do not know how much we have or do not have on a daily basis. This lack of knowledge hurts students and adults tremendously because oftentimes we do not understand bank statements, how to write a check, how debit cards work, etc. For these reasons, along with a host of others, African American students should be required to take at least one or two courses, if not more, on financial literacy. This will make a huge difference in providing a valuable education for all students that will last a lifetime.

Essential Elements of Financial Literacy that Must Be Taught

It is my opinion that there are several essential elements of financial literacy that must be taught in our K-12 schools, particularly in the high school setting. I can't stress enough how critically important this is to prepare the African American student to navigate through this ever-changing global society. I want to categorize these into three main categories: (1) Money Management; (2) Basics of Investing; and (3) Entrepreneurship.

Money Management

It is absolutely essential that African American students learn how to manage the money they have. Before African American students get to this level of understanding, some basic components I discussed earlier in this chapter must be addressed: (1) Assets and Liabilities; (2) Net Worth; (3) Credit Card Management; (4) Checking Account Reconciliation. After these skills are obtained, African American students are ready to understand money management. For this chapter, I am defining money management as the ability to identify, understand, analyze, synthesize and execute the most appropriate related to their own financial situation. In other words, I feel that African American students should gain an understanding of their financial situation at any given time and take the appropriate steps to improve their situation.

We must understand that many African American students are left behind because of 'lack of knowledge' or what I refer to as a 'lack of exposure' to knowledge. Nevertheless, to improve their financial situation, now is the time for them to improve their money management skills. So, African American students must be able to read bank statements and understand the information they provide.

More financial lessons African American students should understand include: the differences between assets and liabilities; how credit cards can help and hurt an individual; how credit works in the United States. More specifically, they must understand how credit cards work. This information is vital because when they become an adult, the credit score will actually become their report card.

African American students must also understand the importance of insurance. These students should have a very good foundational knowledge insurance including term insurance vs. whole life, auto and health insurance. This is vitally important so that when these African American students become adults they will already have acquired this knowledge from school.

In this section of the chapter, I have outlined several key components essential for African American students in the area of money management. To review, they must have a good knowledge base in the following areas:

Key Concepts to Understand for Money Management	
Assets	Liabilities
Net Worth (assets – liabilities)	Credit Card Management
Bank Account Reconciliation	Understanding of Bank Statements
Credit & Credit Scores	Life Insurance
Auto Insurance	Health Insurance

Having a good understanding of each of these key concepts in the field of money management will go a very long way in preparing African American students for the life they will face after completion of high school.

Basics of Investing

As we move forward with this chapter, another important set of concepts critical to a lifetime of financial success for African American students is to understand the basics of investing. The topic of investing can be a book in itself; however, here are a few lessons I feel every student, particularly African

American students, need to know when they graduate from high school.

First, students should have a very good understanding of the *Rule of 72*. The *Rule of 72* is a financial term that helps us understand how fast it takes our money to double itself by the interest rate (another important concept to learn) in different investment vehicles (i.e., certificates of deposits, savings accounts, money market accounts, Treasury Bills, bonds, stocks, etc.). Below, I provide a graph of how long it will take $1,000 to double itself at different interest rates.

72 / interest rate = years

*Illustrates how many years it will take for money to double in value

Second, all students, particularly African American students, need a good understanding of the basics of investing in the stock market. I know there are quite a few schools that teach the concepts of investing in stocks through various stock market games. By learning to invest in the stock market, students can understand how they can own 'shares' of a company and have their money constantly working for them even when they are not doing physical labor.

The third component that students must learn in the world of investing is *cash flow*. Unfortunately, many adults have yet to understand this concept and it ultimately hurts their net worth in the end. Basically, cash flow helps us to understand how much money flows to your pocket after you calculate the income and expenses of the investment. Too often, many adults make these types of investments and they have 'negative' cash flow. Usually, they have to then sell these investments for a much lower price than they are actually worth. As a result, we want African American students to be better prepared to understand this concept when they leave high school.

Real Estate Investing

Another critical concept that students can learn as early as high school is the notion of real estate investing. In teaching this concept, it is important for educators to let students know that adequately learning this skill can change their financial situation for the rest of their lives. I will not go into this in detail in this book; however, we can let students know that people have to live somewhere and they can be the persons who own the places where other people live. I feel that African American students should leave high school with at least a basic knowledge of these concepts.

Entrepreneurship

"Go to school...so you can get a GOOD job." This is a concept that has been taught to so many young people over the years that it is ingrained in the American society. At the time of writing this book, the United States is in a deep 'recession' so many of the 'good jobs' have been lost due to the current economic conditions. As an educator, I do not necessarily have a problem with students going to school to prepare for future employment; however, we should also encourage African American students to become entrepreneurs so they can own their own businesses and create jobs for others as well. Given the foci of this book, I am only briefly addressing this topic. I would encourage every student and every educator to read *Cashflow Quadrant* by Robert Kiyosaki. This book clearly expresses why we should want our students to own businesses and become investors.

Ideally, with all of the current job layoffs, downsizing and bleak economic outlooks, I have plenty of doubts about the *Go to school to get a job* slogan if the jobs are not there. This is why I want us to encourage students to *Go to school so they can start their own businesses.* The reason why I want us to promote this notion is because when these students eventually own their own businesses, they get to make decisions and not be at the mercy of an employer. What I am proposing here is a totally different mindset than how students are taught in schools and in their homes. When African American students have the mindset of a business owner, I think they will use more of their intellectual capital than just being an employee. Let us move forward to change the African American communities by preparing our students to become business owners and investors instead of just employees. Let me say that it is nothing wrong with be an employee if that is what you want to do; however, we must teach our African American students that they can go to greater heights.

Epilogue

It has been a great pleasure to write the 4th edition of this much-needed book. We must understand that African American students, particularly our African American males in our nation's K-12 schools are in a 'state of emergency' (Kunjufu, 2001). If we are going to make a change in their lives, it is critical that we implement the concepts presented in this book. I am an educator who wholeheartedly cares about the future of all students, particularly African American students. It is my sincere hope that because of this book the lives of African American students, many of whom I may never meet personally, may be changed for the better.

Also, I hope this book encourages K-12 educators who labor on the front lines of education seeking advice on what to do to make a difference. Last, I hope this book changes the mindset of some educators that I have met across the United States who are not in this profession for the right reasons. Here is a thought I would like to leave with every educator who reads this book, "When your career in education is over, what kind of grade will you have on your report card from your students?" Stated differently, what impact did you make on the education profession?

I wish all of you the best. Let's make a positive change for African American students in our nation's K-12 schools!